▶ **France Votes**

DOI: 10.1057/9781137356918.0001

Europe in Crisis

Series Editor: **Martin Schain**

The current crisis in Europe has often been depicted as an economic/currency crisis that poses a danger for European economic unity and its common currency, the Euro. Monetary union, it has been argued, has outrun fiscal union, depriving the EU of an important means of dealing with the pressures on the currency. It has also been understood as a crisis of governance, of institutions with the decision-making capacity to deal with the crisis. Finally, the impact of the economic emergency has altered the political landscape in different EU countries in different ways.

The crisis appears to be creating changes that will endure, but cannot yet be predicted entirely. This series fills an important gap in scholarship by supporting a level of analysis that is more thoughtful than the periodic media coverage and less complicated than much of the deep theoretical analysis. These books are timely and concise with the promise of a long lifetime of relevancy.

Titles Include:

Irwin Wall
FRANCE VOTES
The Election of François Hollande

DOI: 10.1057/9781137356918.0001

palgrave▸pivot

France Votes: The Election of François Hollande

Irwin Wall

palgrave
macmillan

DOI: 10.1057/9781137356918.0001

FRANCE VOTES
Copyright © Irwin Wall, 2014.

All rights reserved.
First published in 2014 by
PALGRAVE MACMILLAN®
in the United States—a division of St. Martin's Press LLC,
175 Fifth Avenue, New York, NY 10010.

Where this book is distributed in the UK, Europe and the rest of the world,
this is by Palgrave Macmillan, a division of Macmillan Publishers Limited,
registered in England, company number 785998, of Houndmills, Basingstoke,
Hampshire RG21 6XS.

Palgrave Macmillan is the global academic imprint of the above companies
and has companies and representatives throughout the world.

Palgrave® and Macmillan® are registered trademarks in the United States,
the United Kingdom, Europe and other countries.

ISBN: 978-1-137-35692-5 EPUB
ISBN: 978-1-137-35691-8 PDF
ISBN: 978-1-137-35690-1 Hardback

Library of Congress Cataloging-in-Publication Data is available from
the Library of Congress.

A catalogue record of the book is available from the British Library.

First edition: 2014

www.palgrave.com/pivot

DOI: 10.1057/3981137356918

For Judy

▶

DOI: 10.1057/9781137356918.0001

Contents

DOI: 10.1057/9781137356918.0001

Preface

In spring 2012 I was planning yet another month in Paris
for research in June as had been my practice for the last
ten years, when it dawned on me that France would then
be in the process of voting into office a new National
Assembly, following the presidential elections of May,
which François Hollande, the Socialist, was expected to
win. In my past research, one of the recurrent themes
had been the relationship between French Socialism
and political power; my PhD thesis was originally on
the Popular Front government of Léon Blum, and in the
course of my research I had done studies on the governments of Pierre Mendès France (not a Socialist yet as
prime minister in 1954–1955 but a progressive) and Guy
Mollet, and some peripheral work around the presidency
of François Mitterrand. I conceived the idea of a similar
focus on François Hollande, and I decided to put off the
research I had intended to do and to try to write an article
on the elections of 2012 which I would have the privilege
of witnessing from up close.

I must admit having started with a pre-conceived
hypothesis on "no-choice democracies" that grew out of a
seminar I attended at Columbia University. The term was
meant to apply to the smaller countries in the Eurozone
to which dictation with regard to their financial policies
was being applied by the leadership of the zone, essentially
the Franco-German tandem. But I could not see why the
term should not also be applied to France itself. On the
one hand Hollande was campaigning against austerity:
he promised to restore the zone to policies of growth and

DOI: 10.1057/9781137356918.0002

renegotiate the stability pact that when ratified would lock the Zone into common practices of budget balancing and currency stability, and he called for the issuance of Eurobonds that would at once collectivize and fund the sovereign debt crisis under which the euro, as a currency, was suffering. But on the other hand Hollande continued to promise to balance the French budget and practice austerity in France in order to control inflation, and his program did not contain measures of sufficient reach to enable him to attain his announced goals. In the end it seemed to me he would end up implementing the same polices as his much despised predecessor, Nicolas Sarkozy. The result would be that France would continue to be mired in recession with exceptionally high unemployment, and the economic crisis would continue to aggravate an accompanying political crisis manifested in the rise of a dangerous form of populism in the form of the National Front movement and a growing disaffection between the French population and the political class that governs it. Behind these crises, common to other European nations, lay threats to the European unity project and to the processes of free trade and globalization. I take no pleasure in noting that my fears have largely been confirmed by the outcome during the early years of the Hollande presidency.

In order to conduct my study I rearranged my schedule and contacted some of the leading French political scientists, militants of the various political parties, historian friends, and members of the American Embassy and French Foreign Ministry to request interviews. I must thank all those who responded to my requests and helped make this work better than it would otherwise have been: Pascal Perrineau, Nonna Mayer, Bertrand Badie, Alain Bergounioux, Mark John, Paul Taylor, Noah Barkin, Christopher Klein, Alex Schrank, Thomas Lefebvre, Alexis Dalem, Valérie Lafont, Jeremy Kreins, Eric Roussel, Frédéric Bozo, Philippe Vial, Georges Soutou, Gérard Bossuat, and Robert Frank. In addition, Herrick Chapman played an important role in accepting for publication in *French Politics, Culture and Society* the initial article I wrote on the election, which subsequently became the framework of this book.[1] It was Martin Schain, however, who read the article and first suggested that I try to turn it into a book for the series he was to edit for Palgrave Pivot. Along the way I benefitted from the wise counsel of colleagues who have always been there to help with my work, in particular Kim Munholland, John Sweets, and David Schalk. My dear friend and the translator of my previous books into French, Philippe-Etienne Raviart, did a painstaking reading of the preliminary version of this manuscript and offered sound editing and important suggestions for revision. I thank him profusely for the editing and absolve him, and everyone else, for the errors and weaknesses that remain. All the mistakes are entirely my own. Finally, a special note to my dear wife, Judy Wall—if not for your urging there is no way I would have written the book.

Note

1 Irwin Wall, "France Votes," *French Politics, Culture and Society*, Vol. 30, No. 3 (Fall 2012), 1–20.

DOI: 10.1057/9781137356918.0002

IMAGE 1   *François Hollande, French Socialist party candidate for the 2012 presidential elections, during a press conference in Paris, Wednesday, April 25, 2012, as part of the campaign for the second round of the elections on May 6, 2012. Credit: CHAMUSSY/SIPA/1204251828 (Sipa via AP Images).*

DOI: 10.1057/9781137356918.0002

Introduction

Abstract: *The result of the 2012 election was known before the campaign began. The French president Nicolas Sarkozy suffered unprecedented unpopularity as his country experienced parallel crises. The economy was stagnant while populist parties flourished amid voter disaffection with the political class. François Hollande, the Socialist candidate, offered remedies: he instituted a new system of nation-wide primary elections while dramatically increasing the number of Socialist women candidates for the National Assembly, and he promised to renegotiate the Stability treaty in the Eurozone, ending the draconian austerity that inhibited growth. But Hollande was not up to the task. His proposals were inadequate and his vision limited. France appeared to be a "no-choice democracy."*

Wall, Irwin. *France Votes: The Election of François Hollande.* New York: Palgrave Macmillan, 2014. DOI: 10.1057/9781137356918.0003.

The French election of 2012 initially appeared to have transformative potential in the modern history of France. The anticipated result of the balloting was never in doubt; long before the actual voting took place, polls showed that the Socialist candidate, François Hollande, would be the victor. The incumbent president of the French Republic, Nicolas Sarkozy, had for a long time suffered unusually low ratings in the polls. His austerity policies in dealing with the economic crisis that began in 2008 were widely resented, and his frenetic presidential style and personal behavior were widely criticized. France languished with almost zero economic growth and chronic unemployment.

A long-running process of de-industrialization and transformation to a service economy, with the nation's manufacturing industries being exported abroad at an alarming rate, took place in France in the context of a European Union in crisis. With the exception of Germany and a few smaller north European nations, the EU as a whole suffered static or declining growth and unemployment as a consequence of the recession that began in 2008 in the United States, and there followed very quickly an associated crisis of the common currency, the euro, which was in use in 17 of the 27 nations making up the European Union. The Eurozone severely limited the fiscal options available to its members in dealing with the recession, forcing them into cooperation in the making of decisions, while the institutions for implementing that cooperation had never been constructed. The chaotic process of rescue of near-bankrupt governments fell to hastily improvised conferences, at which the Franco-German tandem led by President Nicolas Sarkozy of France and Chancellor Angela Merkel of Germany, proponents of the new economic orthodoxy of their day, imposed severe policies of austerity on Greece in exchange for bailouts to relieve that nation's excessive sovereign debt. In France reigning president Sarkozy imposed similar policies of austerity on his own nation in a vain attempt to balance the budget as unemployment rates increased and the French economy fell into further recession. Like Clinton in 1992, Hollande in 2012 would come to power on a version of the slogan "It's the economy, stupid" (c'est l'économie, imbécile).

Hollande's candidacy undertook to end the policies of austerity in Europe and to bring about new policies leading to economic growth. To accomplish this he needed to upend the politics of the Eurozone, change the dynamics of the Franco-German partnership, and transform the politics of Europe even as he altered the policies in place in France. His challenge was even greater than that, however, because France itself

DOI: 10.1057/9781137356918.0003

suffered a political crisis corresponding to its economic one. The rise of the nationalist, populist, and anti-immigrant National Front (FN) appeared to represent a threat to the democratic political system; led by Marine Le Pen, the daughter of its charismatic long-time leader Jean-Marie Le Pen, the FN acquired a new dynamism. At the same time a dynamic ex-Socialist, Jean-Luc Mélenchon, led his recently formed Parti de Gauche into an alliance with the historic French Communist Party giving the activist Left a new spurt of popularity. But perhaps more serious than either of those challenges to the established political parties, political scientists noted a growing disaffection between the electorate and the political class as a whole that was reflected in growing abstention rates from election to election. Voters showed widespread distrust of their elected representatives whom they regarded as mired hopelessly in corruption. In a striking parallel, economists warned of growing distrust and quasi-anarchy in employer–employee relations that seriously contributed to the economic crisis and was reflected in the loss of French competitiveness abroad. In the estimation of important analysts, there existed parallel political and economic crises in France that mirrored the growing economic chaos and diplomatic confusion taking place Europe-wide. Hollande was aware of and promised to address all of these crises; to the extent that he would prove able to do so, the elections promised to be truly transformative in the history of France.

This book focuses on François Hollande's election victory, his ambitions, his campaign promises, and his first cautious steps in assuming the apparent formidable powers of the French presidency. It also puts the election in historical context, examining the political forces at play, their historical evolution in recent years, and the role they played in the election outcome. Finally the book puts the election in a Europe wide context, evaluating the importance of the European Union and the Eurozone in the performance of the French economy and the influence of politics and policies in the Eurozone on French decision-makers. In particular the constraints imposed by Europe on French agency in dealing with France's economic problems are emphasized. Since there was little drama to the elections themselves, the outcome of which was in effect known before they were even held, I have adopted a topical rather than chronological approach in what follows. Chapter 1 reviews innovative aspects of the elections, the roles of women and the adoption of primaries in particular, while narrating the run up to the elections. Chapter 2 examines the contending candidates and political forces, in

DOI: 10.1057/9781137356918.0003

particular the National Front. Chapter 3 deals with the campaign and the outcome, Chapter 4 outlines the background of the European Union and the crisis of the euro, and Chapter 5 tries to assess the meaning of it all. A short conclusion depicts the disappointing beginnings of the Hollande presidency.

The French elections, both presidential and legislative, in May and June 2012, were the first essential step in Hollande's trajectory. Beginning with the political crisis, Hollande tried to address voter disaffection even before the elections by modernizing democratic practice in his own party. He began by instituting an expanded primary system in the Socialist party, of which he served as head from 1997 to 2008. He dramatically increased the role of women in the party, capitalizing on the existing system of parity to increase the number of female representatives in the National Assembly while enforcing gender equality in the construction of his government. He promised to reduce the perquisites of deputies to the National Assembly, and once in power he lowered their pay and his own. He vowed to expand local democracy by continued decentralization accompanied by abolition of the hated system of "cumuls," the practice of allowing deputies to combine their national duties with local offices; most deputies in France simultaneously served as mayors and departmental and municipal councilors in their districts giving them outsized power in local politics. Finally Hollande promised to introduce at least a partial electoral system of proportional representation to ensure that the political forces in the country outside the quasi-monopoly of the two governing parties received at least some representation in parliament.

Hollande further promised to address the problems of French youth, education, and pensions while expanding the economy and creating jobs. And he put forth an ambitious social agenda anchored by the promise of gay marriage, *mariage pour tous* meaning marriage for all, and an entirely new code addressing the issues of the modernized family.

Hollande simultaneously undertook to bring a new approach to the problems of the Eurozone. He called first for a transformation of the politics of austerity into policies of growth, and demanded that the Pact of Stability, for the most part already ratified by Eurozone members, be renegotiated so that its strictures on balancing budgets were accompanied by measures to expand economic investment and provide some stimulus for the economy. He counted on his own election victory to

DOI: 10.1057/9781137356918.0003

provide him with a mandate and the clout in Europe to force renegotiation of the treaty upon the recalcitrant Germans. He called for greater economic integration in the Eurozone and common control of the banking system, in crisis in most of the Eurozone countries. In solidarity with the countries facing bankruptcy due to excessive indebtedness, he called for the issuance of Eurobonds, guaranteed by the full faith and credit of the entire Eurozone.

At the time of writing, January 2014, Hollande's popularity had fallen to the lowest levels of any president before him in French history while the French economy appeared to be continuing on its downward spiral. French institutions appeared only marginally if at all transformed, the National Front was on the rise, and the crisis of mass voter disaffection seemed to remain unaddressed. Internationally, stopgap measures appeared to have rescued the euro as a currency, but economic growth in the Eurozone, except in Germany, remained static or in decline.

While examining the politics of reform in France, I hope to reveal in what follows the international, domestic, and personal constraints that appear to have limited the margin of maneuver for François Hollande even as he occupied the uniquely powerful office of the French president, bolstered by majorities for his party in the National Assembly, the Senate, and even the judiciary. Hollande's failure thus far to deal with the crisis in Europe and France is in part a personal failure reflecting his limitations as a leader and the narrowness of his vision. France's uniquely powerful president appears virtually powerless as he attempts to tackle the difficult problems his nation faces. But irrespective of who pretends to lead it, France appears to have become a no-choice democracy. It enjoys full constitutional democratic rights and protections, and the ability to determine for itself the most important of social questions. Certainly by all counts one of Hollande's signal achievements has been the adoption of gay marriage and the associated right of gay couples to adopt children. But with regard to the economy, France has lost its freedom of maneuver with its adherence to the common currency in the Eurozone. By merging its economy with that of the Eurozone it did not get the clout it anticipated in orienting the politics of Europe to its own priorities. At the same time the Europe-wide economic crisis was reflected in political crisis at home in the rise of new political extremism combined with mass disaffection from politics altogether. Once elected, Hollande appeared

DOI: 10.1057/9781137356918.0003

to have changed course and reneged on his campaign promises as he continued to implement the failed policies of his predecessor. And the French appeared to be asking, what good is the people's government if it is powerless to carry out the people's will?

DOI: 10.1057/9781137356918.0003

1
The Innovations

Abstract: *The 2012 election in France occurred under inauspicious circumstances: the Socialists were widely expected to win, but their front-runner, head of the International Monetary Fund, Dominique Strauss-Kahn, was eliminated from contention due to sexual indiscretions. The mantle of candidate fell to the unprepossessing François Hollande, who was aware of a growing crisis in the French political system, characterized by increasing alienation of the voters from the political class that governs them. Hollande rode to the top in the context of efforts by the Socialist party to address that crisis: on the one hand the Socialist party endorsed parity for women and greatly increased their participation in the party, and on the other hand it adopted and expanded the primary system, coming into vogue among many political parties in Europe and Israel. However, these were not sufficient to alleviate the political crisis which is rather driven by divisions in the electorate that transcend the parties, including European unity and globalization.*

Wall, Irwin. *France Votes: The Election of François Hollande.* New York: Palgrave Macmillan, 2014.
DOI: 10.1057/9781137356918.0004.

The French election campaign may be said to have begun curiously in a New York hotel room on May 24, 2011, where the leading potential candidate of the opposition Socialist party (PS), Dominique Strauss-Kahn, who was also serving as head of the International Monetary Fund, was accused of rape by a chambermaid named Nafissatou Diallo. Later that afternoon at JFK Airport, after having boarded his Air France flight to Paris, Strauss-Kahn was arrested by New York City police, held without bail, and subjected to the humiliating "perp walk," a ritual for which New York's finest are famous, before his eventual arraignment by a New York judge. Strauss-Kahn was eventually released on bail, and the case against him collapsed when the interrogation of Ms. Diallo revealed contradictions and possible untruths in her testimony. But his anticipated candidacy for the French presidency was fatally compromised.

Many in France believed that the Socialist leader had been entrapped by President Sarkozy's intelligence services; the assault, if it was that, took place in a French hotel chain, Sofitel, and news of it swept through France immediately, perhaps because of leaks by upper-level hotel personnel, some of whom were seen to react in glee to the news. But even so, a fatal blow had been dealt to Mr. Strauss-Kahn's presidential aspirations. His lame defense against the charges was that he had engaged in "consensual" sex; he could not deny that sex had taken place, however, since the police had discovered his semen strewn on the carpet. If indeed a trap, Strauss-Kahn had fallen into it, and informed circles in France smirked at this apparently most serious of sexual indiscretions for which he already had a reputation in France. The case led to rape charges being brought against him by a young journalist, Christine Banon, based on an incident that allegedly took place eight years earlier, in 2003. Banon accused Strauss-Kahn of attempted rape during an interview she had with him in her capacity as a journalist eight years earlier, explaining that she had been too intimidated to bring charges at the time. Banon's charge was dismissed for lack of evidence and because the statute of limitations had expired, but then revelations emerged of Strauss-Kahn's involvement in orgies and the procuring of prostitutes for a hotel-based sex-ring in the French city of Lille.[1] These charges remained under investigation for the duration of the presidential campaign forcing Strauss-Kahn to withdraw his candidacy.

Diallo's accusation was the first of a series of events that carried François Hollande, a Socialist, to the presidency of France. Hollande seemed an unlikely choice to many, who saw him as an uncharismatic

DOI: 10.1057/9781137356918.0004

career politician. His election still amounted to a minor revolution in French politics given the dimensions of his victory. His victory was unprecedented in its scale, giving him and his party control of the presidency, the National Assembly, the Senate, while it had dominance in the constitutional court; Socialist majorities also already existed in the vast majority of the regions and municipalities throughout France. Hollande appeared ready to use his exceptional mandate from the French people to modify profoundly, if not overturn, the existing relationships of states and power within the European Union. In fact, however, Hollande was perfectly aware, despite appearances, of the limitations on his power; the appearance of Socialist power in France by no means indicated a popular mandate but was rather a peculiar result of the electoral system. And however transformative his policy prescriptions seemed to be, they were limited by his personal timidity and the formidable array of power against them led by the Germans in the policy-making institutions of the European Union. There are several unprecedented aspects to Hollande's victory and to the government he appointed in its wake, however, which are nevertheless transformative in the history of France.

At every French election the question of constitutional change is broached, and 2012 was no exception. Jean-Luc Mélenchon, the candidate of the extreme Left, openly called for a Sixth Republic; Hollande, however, observed that France had no less than 19 constitutions since the Great Revolution of 1789, and he thought that was enough. The Fifth Republic appeared to have become the consensual regime of the French, and Hollande wanted the Socialist party of France once and for all to accept its institutions. France had oscillated between monarchy, republic, and empire throughout its modern history; it seemed to have settled on the Third Republic in 1870, but that regime curiously lacked a constitution, and was rather established by a series of constitutional laws. The Third Republic endured from 1870 to 1940, its institutions gaining a kind of precarious stability and acceptance by the public. But if the institutions were stable the governments were not. The system of a weak president with power vested in a prime minister in need of a majority in the parliament led to chronic governmental instability that was held responsible for the collapse of 1940 and the national humiliation of dictatorship and collaboration under the regime of Marshal Pétain during the Second World War.

After the war, Charles de Gaulle, who was catapulted to the leadership of his country by his heroic leadership of the resistance, tried to establish

DOI: 10.1057/9781137356918.0004

a presidential republic which he proposed to head himself. He failed and went into exile while the Fourth Republic, as pundits pointed out, quickly transformed itself into another version of the Third. De Gaulle bided his time until the Algerian rebellion and the associated political crisis in France presented him with an opening in 1958; his return was regarded as essential to settling the crisis without civil war, but his price was a new constitution and the strong presidency that prevails today.

The system established under the Fifth Republic appeared to work well during de Gaulle's presidency and that of his successors, Georges Pompidou and Valérie Giscard d'Estaing, but with the revival of a united Left during the 1970s threatening to win a majority in the National Assembly, it revealed itself to be less stable than it appeared. In fact the regime had what could have been a fatal flaw. The two-headed executive worked well so long as the president and prime minister were of the same party. But in the event that the Left won the legislative elections of 1978, which for the first time seemed a serious possibility, the president and prime minister would be of opposite parties, with no clear indication of who would actually control the government.

In the event the Socialist-Communist coalition did not win the elections in 1978; instead, François Mitterrand, the Socialist, won the presidency in 1981. The Socialist party, which had long criticized the system for its system of personal power, instead quickly adapted to it once it was able to win the presidency for itself in 1981. Indeed, François Mitterrand, who was the Left's first president in 1981, was the author of a book describing the Fifth Republic as "Le Coup d'État permanent," but as president from 1981 to 1995, through two seven-year terms, he accepted the institutions of the Fifth Republic after all; Mitterrand fitted admirably the role of republican monarch. But when he lost his majority in the National Assembly to the Gaullist Right in the March 1986 legislative elections, the basis of power in the regime again came into question. Mitterrand declined to provoke a constitutional crisis, however, and calmly appointed Jacques Chirac to lead a right-wing government that "cohabited" with the Socialist president from 1986 to 1988. The incipient crisis created by the two-headed executive power was resolved by a partial return to a parliamentary republic. When the Right won again in 1993, Edouard Balladur led a conservative government with Mitterrand as president again in what the French termed a government of "cohabitation." Chirac succeeded Mitterrand as president in 1995 in a return of the conservative Gaullist party to power, but new legislative elections in 1997

DOI: 10.1057/9781137356918.0004

were in turn won by the Left, and Chirac was forced to accept a Socialist-led government headed by Lionel Jospin that lasted for five years from 1997 to 2002. Cohabitation was turning from the exception into the rule as Chirac turned out to be a rather weak president, not at all what de Gaulle, the regime's founder, had envisioned.

Neither of the government parties was satisfied with this situation, and as a consequence in 2002 the system was reformed yet again, this time so that presidential and legislative elections coincided. This reform greatly increased the importance of an already powerful presidency, although the term of sitting presidents was reduced from seven to five years. The 2002 elections were also a huge shock to the system, however: Jean-Marie Le Pen, head of the anti-system National Front party, emerged second to Chirac in the initial balloting for the presidency, nosing out the Socialist challenger, Lionel Jospin, by less than one point, but earning the right to challenge the incumbent president alone in the second round. In the event, Le Pen's candidacy against Chirac in the second round revealed Le pen's isolation as virtually all the other political forces in France rallied to the incumbent president, who received over 80% of the vote on the second ballot. Nevertheless the danger to the system not only from Le Pen but also from the massive disaffection of the voters from the political class in general was apparent for all to see. No single candidate, not even the incumbent President Chirac, could even get beyond 20% of the vote in the first round.

But in 2002 the legislative elections, now held one month after the conclusion of the presidential contest, became a kind of afterthought in which a part of the electorate returned to the polls to ratify its earlier choice and give the president his presidential majority in the National Assembly. After the close of the presidential ballot, the reorganized conservative party, the UMP (*Union pour un Mouvement Populaire*, Union for a Popular Movement), emerged from the legislative elections with a huge majority. Jacques Chirac, newly armed with an 80% majority of the popular vote on the second ballot and a large presidential majority in the National Assembly, in 2002, appeared to be the all-powerful president. But nobody was fooled; France's underlying political crisis was evident as the National Front appeared to threaten the existence of democracy itself. The reform would seem to have minimized if not eliminated the possibility of president and prime minister of opposing parties, but it also diminished the importance of legislative elections in the eyes of French voters. The effect was still all too apparent ten years later in 2012:

DOI: 10.1057/9781137356918.0004

while the participation rate in the presidential balloting in 2012 was among the highest ever recorded in French elections, with over 81% of those registered turning out to vote, the abstention rate in the legislative elections little over a month later set a new record when only 56% of the electorate returned to the polls.[2]

France votes four times in order to accomplish what Americans do with a single day's balloting. Since France has a multi-party system, a second ballot run-off is held to establish the winner following both the presidential and legislative elections. The presidential elections took place on April 22 and May 6, 2012, while the legislative elections were held on June 10 and June 17. There were no less than ten candidates for the French presidency on the first ballot in 2012, and multiple parties contested the first ballot of the legislative elections as well. Nevertheless, François Hollande was able to emerge with an overwhelming victory almost unprecedented in its scale. He won the presidency and an over-whelming majority in the National Assembly, all this despite the fact that the Left, even after one added together all its parts, was still a minority in the country. The fault here lay in the district system of voting as opposed to the more democratic system of proportional representation, which favors the two dominant parties and makes it very difficult for third parties to achieve representation in parliament. Routine in England and America, where two- or three-party systems in the case of England are the rule, this system has been less well digested in France, where strong politically independent forces of the extreme Right and Left, as well as the moderate center, find themselves almost entirely without national representation in parliament. Socialists already before the elections controlled the Senate and most of France's regions and municipalities as well. Now they controlled the presidency and held a solid majority in the National Assembly. But the consequence of this situation was only to make it more difficult for the regime to address the growing sense of political crisis.

Nevertheless it appeared that one aspect of that crisis at least in part had been addressed. Women appeared in substantial numbers in the National Assembly, and Hollande's government, formed immediately after the elections, reflected this: it was the first in French history to include an equal number of men and women as ministers, 17 each for a total of 34 ministers. In addition Hollande found himself dealing with a number of powerful women as he tried to implement his policies: in France, the leader of his own Socialist party, Martine Aubry, and the

DOI: 10.1057/9781137356918.0004

head of the threatening National Front party, Marine Le Pen; and in Europe, the dominant figure Chancellor Angela Merkel of Germany. The appearance of women in politics in a serious way in 2012 reflected years of struggle in France for the feminist demand of parity in political offices, a demand that successfully became enshrined in French law in 2000, if not yet in practice throughout the political system. But if parity was not achieved in the 2012 elections, women have nevertheless emerged as political players in the system to an unprecedented degree; they are today 155 of France's 577 deputies in the French National Assembly.

Hollande's campaign was also characterized by a surprising degree of American influence in the form of institutional borrowing and adaptation, in particular the use of the primary system. His victory occurred despite the fact that the Socialist party was and remains a minority party in France. The combined votes of the Left received a total of less than 45% on the first ballot of the presidential elections. Yet Hollande was able to gain a majority over Sarkozy on the second ballot, while his party achieved one of the most overwhelming political victories in French history in the legislative elections that followed. But despite the dimensions of Hollande's victory, leading political scientists in France interpret his election as further evidence of a national political crisis, manifesting itself in a profound alienation of the population from the political class.[3] The rise of the national-populist and racist National Front party under Marine Le Pen is but one aspect of that crisis. The growing rate of abstentions in French legislative elections is commonly held to be another. And finally, Hollande's election reveals the biggest paradox of all. Despite his unprecedented degree of control over France, his power is severely limited by France's position in the European system. His options as president proved surprisingly narrow, limited by France's European partners, Germany in particular, his own limitations as a politician, and most of all the financial markets. His victory occurred amidst a crisis in the Eurozone, the grouping of 17 nations that since 1999 have adopted and used the euro as their common currency. Embedded economically in the EU and the Eurozone, France, like many of the smaller nations of Europe, has become in many respects a "no-choice" democracy.[4]

Who is François Hollande? Hollande was born into a middle class family of rather right-wing political views. He was educated in a Catholic boarding school, after which he took a degree at France's elite business school, the *Ecole des hautes études commerciales de Paris*. From there he entered the *École Nationale d'Administration*, the training ground for the

DOI: 10.1057/9781137356918.0004

French political and administrative elite. Upon graduation Hollande went almost immediately into politics, slipping easily into the Socialist party that came to power as he graduated. He first worked as an assistant to Jacques Attali, an advisor to President Mitterrand, and then for Jacques Delors, a powerful politician who was expected to be the party's presidential candidate in 1995 following his years at the head of the Commission of the European Union. As a protégé of Delors, Hollande became known as a strong advocate of the European Union. It bears noting that Hollande's Catholic and business-oriented education hardly schooled him in political radicalism, nor did it endow him with the historical perspective or humanist depth of previous French presidents like Mitterrand or Chirac. Although his religious training left him an agnostic, his later penchant for "supply-side socialism" may indicate that he took his business outlook with him into the Elysée.

When Delors withdrew his candidacy for the presidency of France in 1995, Hollande went to work for Lionel Jospin, who ran in Delors's stead. Jospin lost the presidency to Jacques Chirac in 1995, but then became prime minister when the PS won legislative elections in 1997. Jospin did not appoint Hollande a minister, however, but rather preferred to have him at the post of first secretary of Socialist party, in which post Hollande remained for 11 years, until 2008.

That Hollande had never been a minister was held against him during the campaign. As party secretary he did not develop the reputation of being a particularly strong leader either. Hollande is without charisma. Whether he deserves, however, the adjective of "mou," meaning soft, even mushy, that was applied to him, remains questionable. Certainly during the campaign he managed to convince the French that he had the necessary qualities of leadership. But he also was referred to by a journalist as "M. Flanby," the name of a popular dessert pudding, and that appellation stuck through his campaign and has followed him into the presidency. However, Hollande also pursued a career as a deputy in the National Assembly, representing a district in the Department of the Corrèze (also the local base of President Chirac), where he also became president of the Departmental Council and mayor of the city of Tulle. He thus had ample political experience in both national and local politics.

Hollande was secretary of the Socialist party from 1997 to 2008, the longest such tenure in party history. He left his position after the defeat of the party candidate, Ségolène Royal, in the elections of 2007, for which he was in part held to blame. Hollande's tenure as secretary was

DOI: 10.1057/9781137356918.0004

not particularly dynamic, but the party did well in local elections under his leadership, and it appeared poised to win the presidency too when Chirac's second term ended in 2007. This was to overlook, however, the dynamism of Nicolas Sarkozy at the head of the re-formed conservative UMP. Moreover, Hollande's enthusiasm for Europe had embarrassed the PS in 2005 and led to the most serious mistake of his period as party secretary. With a referendum on a proposed European constitution coming up in 2005, Hollande, confident of its passage, thought it benefi-cial to first put the PS on record in favor of the European constitution, and he called an internal party referendum on the draft in December 2004, before the national referendum that took place in 2005. Hollande may have been seeking as well to undermine the future presidential candidacy of Laurent Fabius, who had declared his opposition to the European constitutional project. By putting the party on record in favor of the constitution, Fabius's position was weakened. The referendum in the party did put it on record in favor of the European constitution, but by a smaller majority than anticipated, and the extent of Hollande's miscalculation became clear when the nation as a whole repudiated the treaty, embarrassing the PS which had just voted in its favor. Hollande's expectation of being the party's candidate in 2007 was dealt a blow, and he stepped aside in the face of Ségolène Royal's successful primary campaign among party members.

The Royal candidacy was a surprise to everyone in the party, even to Hollande, despite the fact that their personal relationship as life-companions, in an Anglo context one might say common-law marriage, dated back over 25 years. Hollande and Ségolène Royal had four children together. She was at the same time the first of a group of powerful women in French politics, whose emergence in part reflected the law establishing the goal of parity between men and women in politics passed in France in 2000. Her rise also reflected a peculiar mixture of the personal and political in France that became characteristic of the Hollande presidency as it had been during the term of his predecessor, Nicolas Sarkozy. Hollande and Royal were moving toward estrangement in their relation ship by 2005, however, when she broached her candidacy for president of the Republic. She was the first president of a major French region and a dynamic personality, attractive in appearance: her popularity caught on with party militants, allowing her rapidly to bypass so-called party elephants like Laurent Fabius and Dominique Strauss-Kahn who were obvious presidential aspirants. Fabius had been prime minister under

DOI: 10.1057/9781137356918.0004

Mitterrand, and Strauss-Kahn had been finance minister under Lionel Jospin. Few at the time seemed to regard Hollande, who had never been a minister, as presidential material in any case.

Following the defeat of Royal, Hollande stepped down as party secretary, a position he had held too long and that clearly would not provide the best path to his party's presidential nomination. The party's presidential nominee was to be chosen by an open primary, the first such in the party's history, scheduled to take place in October 2011. Defeated for the presidency by Sarkozy in 2007, Royal decided to stand for the position of party secretary herself to replace Hollande. She appeared to assume that the position was hers by right, and that she would be the presumptive candidate for the presidency in 2012 as well. Defeat in elections rarely resulted in the forced retirement of politicians in France as is the case in the United States: Mitterrand and Chirac had both been defeated several times before finally being elected to the presidency. Royal thought to follow their example, but the circumstances had now changed, and she was at once challenged for the party leadership by another powerful woman in the PS leadership, Martine Aubry. By seeking the party leadership Aubry was evincing presidential ambitions herself, but she also represented the ambitions of the other powerful party figures who had wanted the nomination in 2007, Fabius and Strauss-Kahn, and who had resented Royal's candidacy. They rallied to Aubry's support.

It is quite likely that the struggle between the two women for the leadership of the Socialist party weakened them both; the press had a field day with it, characterizing it as "la guerre des dames," or "sororicide." Aubry enjoyed an electoral base in the Nord as mayor of Lille. She was the daughter of noted PS statesman Michel Delors, who had headed the European Economic Community during the dynamic years of ever greater unity in the 1980s and who was expected to be the PS presidential candidate in 1995. Hollande, as earlier noted, was a protégé of Delors, whose enthusiasm for the European project he shared. This relationship extended by implication to Aubry; he was thus connected to both of the women who were battling for the party leadership. Royal was his former life partner, and Aubry a kind of sister, for if she was Delors's biological daughter, Hollande was Delors's spiritual son. Hollande did not take sides in their struggle for the party leadership, which enabled him later to deal equally with both Royal and Aubry. The PS defeat in the 2007 presidential elections certainly had more to do with Sarkozy's strength and Royal's weakness as candidates, and could not in any sense be attributed

DOI: 10.1057/9781137356918.0004

to Hollande's 2005 blunder. But when Aubry wrested the position of party secretary from Royal in 2008, she joined Royal, Strauss-Kahn, and Fabius as likely presidential candidates of the PS, making it seem further unlikely that Hollande could get the nomination for himself.

The three appear to have decided upon Strauss-Kahn as their preferred candidate, leaving Hollande to his own devices. As an economist amidst a new depression that began in 2008, Strauss-Kahn was thought the best equipped among the opposition to Sarkozy to deal with the crisis. His position as head of the International Monetary Fund gave him a kind of "star" quality in common with Sarkozy. Since the crisis of 2008 and then after the onset of the euro crisis in 2010, Strauss-Kahn could be seen in the company of world leaders at various gatherings such as the Eurozone heads of state or the G 20; and he became a prominent figure in the meetings devoted to the Greek sovereign debt crisis in which the IMF acted in concert with the European Central Bank and the European Commission. In those meetings Strauss-Kahn voiced a policy of moderation as compared to the chorus of stringent advocacy of austerity coming from EU sources led by Germany, warning that Eurozone nations in crisis could not be squeezed lest they reach a breaking point. He gained a reputation for good sense even as he was ignored. Strauss-Kahn's marriage to France's leading television journalist, the independently wealthy and glamorous Anne Sinclair, also served to make him part of a dynamic duo of wealth and fame that rivaled Sarkozy's glitz, while his mixture of East-European and Moroccan Jewish ancestry matched Sarkozy's exotic appeal as well. Among political insiders in France, Strauss-Kahn was also known as a "dragueur," however, the French term for a Don Juan, someone who was always on the prowl for sexual encounters with pretty women. But this issue lay in abeyance, considered of little importance by many of the same people who admired his economic insights and political skills.

Strauss-Kahn's apparent popularity and favored status as presidential candidate raises interesting questions, indeed, about widely alleged anti-Semitism of the French. The French would seem to have chosen Strauss-Kahn as the party's presidential candidate, or perhaps the press did so with the public following suit, but polls showed very early that Strauss-Kahn was emerging as the PS's top candidate in the period from 2008 to 2011 despite his Jewishness. Anne Sinclair also was issue of a prominent Jewish family, and their marriage, Strauss-Kahn's third, was performed by a Rabbi. Nor did the Jewish question, if that term is still apt, come up

DOI: 10.1057/9781137356918.0004

during the incidents leading to Strauss-Kahn's disgrace, except among dark recesses of the internet.[5] Strauss-Kahn himself raised the issue of his possible weaknesses as a presidential candidate during this time, citing both his Jewishness and his reputation as a ladies' man. Ironically it was the latter that did him in. But as the Socialist primary of October 2011 drew near Strauss-Kahn ran ahead of everyone else in the polls as a possible candidate against Sarkozy, and both Aubry and Fabius thought it unwise to oppose him. With the obvious precedent of the victory of Barak Obama on everyone's mind, the slogan "Yes we Kahn" started to make the rounds.[6] Aubry preferred to subordinate her own candidacy to make way for Strauss-Kahn, expecting that once elected president, he would make her prime minister, while Fabius appeared likely to be his minister of foreign affairs.

Lacking in charisma, Hollande did not even suggest himself to the others as the next presidential candidate, but he calmly pursued his own ambition nevertheless, undeterred by Strauss-Kahn's greater popularity. He lost 20 kilos under the guidance of his new love, the journalist Valérie Trierweiler of *Paris-Match*, and he purchased a new wardrobe of stylish clothing. Coached by Valérie Trierweiler he made a careful study of the mannerisms and gestures of his predecessor as Socialist president of France, François Mitterrand, whom Hollande succeeded in imitating if he failed, nevertheless, to exude Mitterrand's natural charisma and authority.[7] He was thus well-positioned to take up the mantle that Strauss-Kahn had ignominiously abandoned following the sordid incident in the New York branch of Sofitel in May 2011.

The 2007 presidential election saw the first female candidate of one of the major governing parties of France; Ségolène Royal, the Socialist party candidate, was defeated by Nicolas Sarkozy on the second ballot by 53% as against 47%. But it was the 2012 presidential and legislative elections that marked the definitive emergence of women on the French political scene. The entry of women to the highest echelons of French politics is in part a consequence of the law of November 6, 2000, that legislated parity between men and women in the French political system. The law made parity a goal rather than a requirement in French politics; it obliged political parties to observe parity in the numbers of their candidates to elective offices, but the law did not mandate parity among those actually elected. That would have been considered a violation of democracy. The initial results of the law immediately after its passage were deceiving, and it seemed to have no effect on the 2002 elections.

DOI: 10.1057/9781137356918.0004

The existing male-dominated parties were left to their own devices as to whether to field women candidates and if so, in which districts to place them, or where on their lists in the case of proportional representation to put them. For a variety of reasons, electoral, institutional, or ideological, resistance to female candidacies manifested itself in most of the parties, and most importantly, the major government parties. Thus in 2002, only 12% of the National Assembly were women, despite the requirement of parity in candidates, and in 2007 the number improved only slightly to 18.5%. Only in the 2012 elections did 155 women take their seats in the 577 seat National Assembly of France, more than a quarter of that body if not yet near a half. This may rank as a breakthrough for France, but it still ranks the nation only 37th among nations of the world in terms of the participation of women in politics.

The parties could also avoid implementing the law by paying a fine, and the conservative UMP consistently chose to pay the fines rather than to field female candidates because it feared they would lose. It was further believed among militants of almost all the parties, most of whom remain men, that female candidates would be more likely to lose elections, although this statistically cannot be shown to have been the case.[8] Another serious impediment to the parties choosing women as candidates was their preference to keep running incumbents, the vast majority of whom were men, because incumbency was always a distinct advantage over challenger status in electoral contests. These restraints on women have prevented parity from being achieved, although there has been substantial progress for women both in local politics and nationally. But if parity remains a goal rather than an achievement still in 2012, its pursuit nevertheless has led to dramatic progress in terms of the numbers of women in politics generally and their presence in key positions of power on the national scene.

The 1970s constituted a turning point in which female voting behavior, which traditionally had favored the Right (women tended to be more religious than men), began to shift to the Left. On the one hand society became more secular and religion became less important in terms of determining voting behavior; on the other hand women's social issues such as contraception, divorce, and abortion achieved increased salience as the women's movement worked its way into popular consciousness. The Socialist party decided early that to champion these issues would be a winning strategy. The party imposed quotas for female candidates in offices: 10% of its candidacies were reserved for women in 1974, 15%

DOI: 10.1057/9781137356918.0004

in 1977, 20% in 1979, 30% in 1990, and 40% of party nominations were reserved for women by the year 2000 when parity was deemed to have been achieved. The Socialists were in the process of applying parity in their choice of candidates even before the law took effect.

The Socialist party was further spurred on to action on the women question since it seemed not only a winning strategy but a response to the growing sense of popular alienation from politics; more women in politics would make the political class look more like the civil society from which it emerged.

Prior to the adoption of the parity law France had once of the worst records from the standpoint of female participation in politics in Europe. Since the adoption of parity as a goal the French record with regard to women's participation in politics has changed dramatically. Surprisingly, parity was implemented without much of a struggle; once the Socialists championed it the parties of the Right either would not or felt that they could not oppose it, and no sooner was it adopted as a goal in the early 1990s than they all endorsed it. The idea of parity was first proposed at a European women's conference in Athens in 1992, and it was quickly adopted by the women's movement in France immediately thereafter. It was thrust into public consciousness by the presidential elections of 1995, and it was a striking evidence of the evolution of public opinion on the issue when it turned out that the two major candidates for the presidency in 2005, Jacques Chirac and Lionel Jospin, both decided to endorse it. Chirac won the 1995 elections, but by 1997 his conservative government had been defeated in new elections for the National Assembly, and Lionel Jospin was able to form a Socialist government of "cohabitation" that pushed the parity law through the National Assembly.

The biggest obstacle to parity came not so much from the Right but rather the moderate intellectual Left, and whether or not it was appropriate became debate fodder for two of France's most important feminist intellectuals, Elizabeth Badinter and Sylviane Agacinski. Interestingly both had political ties: Elizabeth Badinter's husband Robert Badinter was the former head of France's Constitutional Court during the presidency of Mitterrand, while Agacinski was the wife of the prime minister and head of the PS before Hollande, Lionel Jospin. The issue was framed in a typically French way; the French have been hostile to American style multiculturalism, refusing to recognize ethnic groups as other than citizens in the abstract, and they have adamantly refused to see any connection between demands of women and minority groups.

DOI: 10.1057/9781137356918.0004

Quotas and affirmative action in France were formally outlawed by the Constitutional Council in 1982 as contrary to France's universal definition of citizenship. What is lauded in the United States as "multiculturalism" is typically denounced in France as "communautarisme," a threat to "Frenchness," a quality that is independent of ethnicity and is taken to denote adherence to a civilization and a set of democratic and lay values to which any member of a different ethnic group can assimilate. Sex, however, is independent of social class or ethnicity, and advocates of parity specifically rejected any comparison of their demands with campaigns in favor of quotas or affirmative action. Sexual equality, they argued, could not be reduced to the struggle of ethnic or racial groups for ethnic equality or inclusion. Nor do women have the option of ethnic groups to assimilate. Sexual identity is rather a feature of humanity in the abstract, intrinsic to it, a product of biology, not culture. The problem for traditionalists like Badinter was that the status of citizen, whether citoyen or citoyenne historically, masculine or feminine, at least after women were given the right to vote, was meant to apply to human beings in the abstract, independently of sex. Badinter further argued that enforced parity was patronizing if not in its own way paternalist, implying that women were incapable of achieving equality on their own. But critics of Badinter's position, led by Agacinski, argued that humanity in the abstract independently of sex did not exist, and therefore universal citizenship could make no sense conceptually either. To conceive of humanity in the abstract was traditionally to conceive of the male human form. The framers of the "Declaration of the Rights of Man and Citizen," moreover, had only men in mind. Human beings cannot be conceived of independently of their sexuality. They are anatomically dual, they come in two varieties, men or women, and the only way to achieve equality among them is to recognize that fact. Once this was done, Agacinski argued, the rest followed: for there to be human equality there had to be political equality among the sexes, and to achieve that it was necessary to impose parity on men and women in their bids for public office.[9]

The major political parties were held responsible by the law to field as many women as men as candidates for political office, in all elections, national and local, with the exception of Departmental Councils. As a result, Departmental Councils until today remain bastions of male supremacy; nationally in 2012 they contained only 13.8% women. The political parties all reacted differently to parity. France's conservative party, the UMP, subordinated legal obligations to electoral considerations

DOI: 10.1057/9781137356918.0004

in implementing the law; it would not unseat incumbents, mostly men, who almost routinely were re-nominated in districts where they already held their seats, and despite a centralized structure, its Political Bureau declined to overrule local instances of the party if they preferred male candidates. Although the party had voted for parity in 2000, it did so for electoral reasons, but it remained ideologically opposed to it, and the party refused to nominate women where it thought they might make weaker candidates than men. Or put another way, the qualifications for candidacy, being well known, devoting years to loyal party work, serving otherwise in local offices, particularly as mayor of larger cities and town, tended otherwise to be inherently gender biased. The penalty for not fielding enough women candidates was also, for a large party like the UMP, not a sufficient deterrent. Fines were levied on the parties proportionately to their failure to field an equal number of female candidates. But subsidies to the political parties in France by the state are distributed according to the number of votes the party receives and the number of deputies it manages to elect. The UMP regarded it as being more cost effective to elect a man and receive the additional subsidy than to lose with a woman and not have to pay the fine. This despite evidence that when women do run in France they tend to do as well as men.[10] In 2012 the UMP ran women in less than 30% of the districts and for the most part in districts that it considered itself likely to lose in any case. Consequently only 14% of its deputies, only 27 deputies of a total of 188 in the National Assembly elected in 2012, are women, despite the law on parity.

In contrast the PS balanced ideological and electoral considerations in implementing the law, striving to fulfill its obligations as much as possible while trying at the same time not to lose seats unnecessarily. For Socialists, equality for women was simply an extension of the party's quest for political and economic equality. The party had gone on record as endorsing women's rights since Mitterrand in the 1980s, and it considered its feminist advocacy as both moral and a winning issue at the same time. However the PS, like the UMP, could not and would not ignore the prior claim of incumbents to run again, and also believing in some cases men more likely to win than women, tended to field female candidates also in districts it thought itself likely to lose in any case. In consequence, although it ran close to 50% women, it elected women as only 37% of its parliamentary group, 104 women of a total of 280 total PS deputies. The other parties of the Left, further Left than the PS, the Front de Gauche and the Ecologists (EELV), strictly observed parity out of ideological

DOI: 10.1057/9781137356918.0004

reasons; most interestingly the Greens fielded an equal number of female and male candidates despite the party being made up of a clear majority of men. They elected nine women and nine men. The Front de Gauche, however, elected mainly Communists and most of them incumbents; its parliamentary delegation is composed of ten deputies only two of whom are women. The most interesting case is that of the FN. Led by a woman, the FN espouses patriarchal hegemony, opposing abortion and espousing a state-granted maternal salary for women who devote their lives to having children and caring for them. The party is otherwise dominated by men and supported mostly by male voters. But it observes parity strictly in fielding candidates because, although its subsidy is substantial for 19% of the vote, it cannot afford to lose any funding by having to pay the fines. In 2012 it elected three deputies, two male and one female, the woman being the niece of Marine Le Pen.

It was the PS that implemented the law first, and the PS was first to nominate a woman as its presidential candidate in 2007. The irony was that she was the most powerful and influential woman in Hollande's personal life—his former life partner and mother of his children (he has never married), Ségolène Royal. In French politics it has been impossible for either of the major parties to separate the personal and the political. Royal, a politician in her own right and president of one of France's largest regions (Poitou-Charentes), surprised Hollande and most of the Socialist party leaders by winning the party's primary election and capturing the nomination in 2007. She was the only female president yet to emerge among France's regions, itself an indication of the limited progress parity had made from its inception in 2000 to the elections of 2007. But women had made significant progress in municipal and departmental elections by 2007 as well as in national contests. In the 2007 elections nationally 107 women were elected to the National Assembly, more than twice the number that were elected in 2002, and in the elections of 2012, 155 women took their seats in France's highest legislative body. The latter figure pushed the number of women above 25% (there are 577 total seats in the Assembly) even if it was still far short of parity.

The irony in the appearance of Ségolène Royal on the national political scene lay in the fact that from the beginning the political candidacy of women became bound up with their personal lives. Royal was the life companion of François Hollande who as secretary of the Socialist party had his eye on the presidential nomination for himself; although never stated, it was thought by many to be understood that the titular head

DOI: 10.1057/9781137356918.0004

of the party would have claim on its candidacy for president. But Royal had proved the more popular of the two among party militants, and Hollande was forced to step aside for her, support her, and campaign at her side. This was complicated in turn by the fact that Hollande somewhat earlier had begun an affair with a rather glamorous journalist for *Paris-Match*, Valérie Trierweiler, which he carried on in secret during the campaign. Only after Royal's defeat by Nicolas Sarkozy in the 2007 election did Royal signal her awareness of the affair and throw Hollande out of their apartment. Trierweiler, who had covered the "Royal couple" of the Socialist party for her magazine and had become a friend of the family, became for Hollande the new "love of his life." She was to accompany him on his trajectory toward the Elysée palace in 2012 and become France's "First Lady." Unfortunately her jealous rivalry with Royal later emerged to trouble the campaign and the outset of Hollande's presidency. And ironically, according to some later speculation, Hollande had already begun yet another affair even as she began what turned out to be her very short tenure as First Lady of France.

Ségolène Royal's candidacy in 2007 was hardly free of gender bias, exaggerated perhaps by the fact that she was regarded as attractive, photogenic, and hence wonderful press copy. Her appearance consequently became the subject of news coverage, frequently obscuring what she had to say. Her apparel was carefully noted after every public appearance.[11] Gender bias also crept into reportage, in particular when her competence to be president was questioned; this is not to judge whether she was or was not competent to be president—competence was not listed in the constitution as a qualification for the job—but merely to note that the issue of competence was rarely posed for male candidates. She was also judged to be emotional in her debate with Sarkozy; in short she could not escape feminine stereotyping, whether or not it played a role in causing her defeat at the polls.

If Royal's candidacy mixed the personal with the political, the admixture became the hallmark of her opponent's presidency. Like his opponent, Sarkozy was in a problematic marriage at the time of his presidential candidacy. His wife Cécelia, who once had been his chief political adviser, had left him for another man, Richard Attias, a businessman whom she later married. Her departure in 2005 caused Sarkozy much pain—he appears to have genuinely loved her—but she agreed to return prior to the elections and campaigned at his side. She showed no interest in the job of First Lady, however, and appeared to find life at the Elysée

DOI: 10.1057/9781137356918.0004

palace a kind of imprisonment. She did play a prominent diplomatic role in July 2007 at her husband's request, flying to Tripoli in order to negotiate the release of five Bulgarian nurses and a Palestinian doctor whom the mercurial dictator Gaddafi had charged with deliberately infecting Libyans with the HIV virus. But by October 2007 she had left Sarkozy, whose position as president of the Republic could not shield him from the humiliation of seeing his wife leave him and marry her former lover.

As president, however, Sarkozy bounced back rather quickly. In November 2007 he met Carla Bruni at a dinner at the Elysée, and he married her in February 2008. Although the marriage was widely seen as a manifestation of his taste for celebrity—Bruni was a successful fashion model who switched careers to become a hit popular singer—she settled into the role of First Lady while bearing Sarkozy a son.

With Strauss-Kahn out of the running, the major obstacle on the road to Hollande's capture of the Socialist party nomination was another powerful woman, Martine Aubry. The Hollande-Aubry contest in their primary was relatively free of the kind of gender bias the press had shown in the 2007 election. This may have been the result of Aubry's lack of luster as an example of femininity, although she did attract the sobriquet of "authoritarian woman," as if in some sense women and authority were or should be contradictory in terms. Aubry was acerbic, and it was she who attacked Hollande as "mou," which means soft, but when applied to a person can mean languid, even indolent or spineless. She argued that given the existence of a "hard" Right in France the country could not afford a "Socialisme mou," a soft or feeble Left. Hollande replied that he did not know what "hard" Socialism might be; he thought in terms of solidarity and firmness tempered by compassion. Aubry's intemperate attacks on Hollande did not appear to hurt his candidacy once the primary was over, but they probably cost her the job of prime minister, which she coveted after Hollande's election.

But the woman who put Hollande into the presidency was Marine Le Pen. A deceptively clever politician, who disarmingly might pass for the ebullient housewife next door, Le Pen succeeded her father as the head of France's right-wing National Front party in January 2011 and immediately started the party on an upswing that carried her to 17.9% of the vote on the first ballot of the 2012 elections for the presidency.[12] This was an unprecedented high vote total for the National Front, which together with the conservative UMP party of President Sarkozy and the Center party, in fact, made up the majority of the French electorate. Le

DOI: 10.1057/9781137356918.0004

Pen's aim, however, was not to reelect Sarkozy but rather to defeat him, in the hope of leading her National Front to the point of displacing the UMP altogether as the leading party of the French Right. Consequently, following the first ballot of the presidential election, she pointedly refused to endorse Sarkozy in the run-off, leaving her supporters free to vote according to their own consciences, and opening the way to Hollande's election. Even had she endorsed Sarkozy, many of her voters might still have preferred Hollande to the UMP leader.

Finally, the most powerful woman of them all, Angela Merkel, chancellor of Germany, remained to be confronted once Hollande became president of France. In her hands lay the determination of whether Hollande would be able to succeed as president in the short run, and she alone appeared to have the power to make the euro and the European Union surmount the current sovereign debt crisis. Merkel originally opposed Hollande's election. She never liked Sarkozy either, but she established a working relationship with him, and he eventually yielded to her in his desire to share a joint role in the direction of the Eurozone if not the European Union. Merkel declared her public support for Sarkozy's reelection early in February 2012. Sarkozy asked her not to receive Hollande during his visits to Germany lest she appear to be entertaining the possibility of his victory, and she acceded to Sarkozy's request. During the campaign *Le Monde* accused her of heading a reactionary cabal of European leaders, a "holy alliance," no less, against Hollande. This was perhaps exaggerated, but Merkel quickly revealed the limits of Hollande's power by scotching his proposal for Eurobonds. She alone appeared to hold the key to the future success of his government.

Hollande is not a figure who naturally exudes authority or power, and being surrounded by exceptionally powerful women probably has not helped his image either. The issue of his personal life was to follow him into his presidency when he dropped Valérie Trierweiler in favor of yet another woman a year and a half into his term. The unofficial biographers of Valérie Trierweiler describe him as unable to say "yes" to Trierweiler (who would have liked to marry him), unable to say "no" to Ségolène Royal, unable to say either yes or no to Martine Aubry, and unable to say anything at all to Angela Merkel. As it turned out he had a great deal to say to Merkel after the election, but he was powerless to influence her.

The appearance of women among the political class, it was hoped, would make the politicians more like the citizens who elected them. This was one way to address the political crisis. But the PS also sought to bring the citizens closer to the actual functioning of politics; the means to do this was the expansion of the primary system. Ironically the primary system has been the means by which the United States may be said to have genuinely expanded democracy in the world in the recent period.[13] The French Socialists have been experimenting with the primary system since 1995. It was initially adopted by the Italian Left, but has come full circle through the political spectrum; even Marine Le Pen became leader of the French National Front following a primary in that party in January 2011. French political parties are small in membership by American, German, or British standards: by instituting an open primary in 2011 the French Socialists hoped to gain legitimacy as the leading party of the opposition, increase their membership, and achieve a great deal of publicity. The Italian Center-Left party held a successful primary election in October 2005, won by Romano Prodi. In 2008 Terra Nova, the French Left think tank, sent observers to study the primary system in the United States and the electoral techniques successfully used by Barack Obama. They urged the Socialists to follow suit in France. By means of its 2011 primary the PS managed to expand dramatically popular participation in its politics: a party that rarely has exceeded 200,000 in membership in its history managed to garner 2.9 million people to participate in its primary, a sign of its conversion to an American-style catch-all party.[14] In the 2007 primary, only formal party members had been allowed to vote, resulting in the victory of Ségolène Royal and the subsequent marginalization of Hollande. In the October 2011 party primary, which was open to anyone who wanted to participate, Hollande got his revenge. He won handily, defeating Party Secretary Martine Aubry on the first ballot and again on the second ballot run-off, while Ségolène Royal suffered the humiliation of coming in fourth place.

During the campaign preceding the run-off, Hollande and Aubry held three debates, all of which were televised by one of the major channels despite protests by the UMP. The debates attracted in the vicinity of three million viewers and were regarded as a great success. Hollande thus had some cachet and legitimacy as the popular choice of a considerable number of voters when he ran in 2012. After the first ballot of the primary, moreover, the other candidates who had tried their luck, Ségolène Royal, Manuel Valls, and Arnaud de Montebourg, all rallied to his support. Aubry finally rallied to him as well after her defeat on the second ballot of the primary. This further legitimated Hollande's candidacy and endowed it with some prestige as he challenged the incumbent

DOI: 10.1057/9781137356918.0004

president Sarkozy. The UMP, which had earlier derided the Socialists for their Americanization in adopting the primary system, seriously began to consider adopting a primary itself to choose its candidate in 2017.

The participation of women in politics, and the open primary, were ends in themselves, but were meant also to contribute to the solution, or at least the mitigation, of what appears to some political scientists to be a profound crisis of democracy in France, in which "civil society" so to speak, meaning broadly the electorate, appears to be increasingly alienated from the political class as a whole, if not the system itself. As mentioned, the growing abstention rate in elections and the rise of the National Front are usually seen as the prime evidence. There is a deeper opposition, however, between the public and the politicians in France that is unaddressed, and that could ultimately pose an even more serious threat to political stability in the future. The French political class, here meaning the governing parties of the UMP and the PS, both believe strongly in the necessity of the construction of Europe. The French public is divided on this issue, but it seems clear after the defeat of the proposal for a European constitution in 2005 that a majority of the French do not want further European integration.[15] And the party that systematically opposes the construction of European Union is the National Front.

While building economic Europe the French have rejected political federalism, championed by their German partners, in deference to the strictures that President de Gaulle, the founder of the Fifth Republic, insisted upon on behalf of French independence and sovereignty. De Gaulle's vision for Europe was rather that of inter-governmentalism, in which each state would exercise a veto power, and this dogged insistence has led to the emergence of the European Council, consisting of heads of government, as a superior power in the structure of the EU, over the European Commission, which was originally envisioned as the real European executive power by treaty founders in 1956.[16] Historically the French have always been ambivalent about Europe. While they have tried to organize Europe around French foreign policy prescriptions of Gaullist independence, they have tried at the same time to use Europe as a projection of French power. These goals are in some measure contradictory.

The French population, however, tends to distrust Europe altogether, and has upset the politicians on two occasions. In 1992 it very narrowly approved the Treaty of Maastricht, which provided for the establishment of the euro, in a referendum that was expected to win overwhelmingly, and it emphatically rejected the proposal for a European "constitution"

DOI: 10.1057/9781137356918.0004

in another referendum in 2005.[17] Both votes remained without any meaningful consequences, however, and European leaders later went on to implement the Maastricht Treaty, which provided for the eventual adoption of the euro, and some aspects of the project for a constitution as well, despite its rejection by voters in the Netherlands and France. The division over Europe straddles the traditional divide between Right and Left in France and lies rather within the governing parties, leaving them both divided on the issue. It is also linked with globalization, behind which lurk the threats of Americanization and immigration, and more vaguely with the issues of extreme liberalism (feminism, multiculturalism, and gay marriage) that have opened new cleavages in the French body politic.[18] These issues further drive the continued rise in popularity of the National Front. This was demonstrated most clearly among an estimated 10–12% of French voters who normally lean neither Right nor Left in elections. These voters tend to be economically precarious (almost 70%), and hence they favor some national redistribution of wealth, which attracts them to the Left; however they are also protectionist and anti-immigrant, suspicious of the euro and hostile to globalization, which draws them toward the Right. It is difficult for them to reconcile their leftist tendencies with Europe and globalization.[19] In the final analysis many of them opt for a nationalistic style of socialism.

This suggests that Socialist party's efforts to democratize the system, both by advancing women and holding primaries, are not likely to fully address the political crisis, which is rather driven by the cleavage in France between adherents and critics of the European project. Neither of the major governing parties, moreover, Socialists and UMP, is able to give expression to that cleavage. It is further an open question whether the opposition to Europe, and behind Europe the specter of globalization, is driven in turn by traditional notions of national sovereignty or by the sense that the European and international systems both conspire to force France into the straitjacket economic policies summed up in the word "austerity." If true this would suggest that if Hollande wished to simultaneously save the European project and address the crisis in the French political system he would need to bring about the fundamental reorientation of economic policies in the EU and the Eurozone that his campaign promised. This in turn suggests that it was not the outcome of the election that really mattered; from the outset it was clear that Hollande was overwhelmingly likely to win. It was rather how Hollande would use that victory on which the future of Europe, and perhaps democracy itself in France, might depend.

DOI: 10.1057/9781137356918.0004

Notes

1   Strauss-Kahn admitted to sexual harassment, however, for which he could not be prosecuted because of the statute of limitations. See Raphaëlle Bacqué and Ariane Chemin, *Les Strauss-Kahn* (Paris: Albin Michel, 2012). On the idea of a conspiracy against Strauss-Kahn, see Edward Jay Epstein, "What Really Happened to Strauss-Kahn," *The New York Review of Books*, December 22, 2011.

2   Anne Muxel, in Pascal Perrineau, *La Décision électorale en 2012* (Paris: Armand Colin, 2013), p. 86.

3   Bertrand Badie, personal interview, June 13, 2012; Pascal Perrineau, personal interview, June 26, 2012.

4   The phrase was the title of a Roundtable held at the Blinken Institute, Columbia University, April 23, 2012: "No Choice Democracies: How the Deep Crisis of Europe is Destroying the Community Model."

5   "The Strauss-Kahn Affair and France's Jews," *Haaretz*, May 25, 2011.

6   *France Today* (French news in English), March 16, 2011, has an excellent summary of the Strauss-Kahn boom candidacy.

7   Anne Mansouret, *Chronique d'une victoire avortée* (Paris: Jean-Claude Gawsewitch, 2011). The title appears to be meant as a warning to Hollande to change his behavior lest he suffer the humiliation of Jospin in 2002 and fail even to make the run-off election. Mansouret is the mother of Christine Banon, who brought the rape charge against Strauss-Kahn based on the incident of 2003; she also had a brief affair with Strauss-Kahn herself.

8   Katherine Opollo, *Gender Quotas, Parity Reform, and Political Parties in France* (Lanham, MD: Lexington Books, 2006).

9   The debate is elucidated in Joan Scott, *Parité* (Chicago: University of Chicago Press, 2005).

10   Rainbow Murray, *Parties, Gender Quotas, and Candidate Selection in France* (Paris: Palgrave Macmillan, 2010).

11   Rainbow Murray, "Progress But Still No Presidente: Women and the 2012 French Presidential Elections," *French Politics, Culture and Society* Vol. 30, No. 3 (Winter 2012), 45–59.

12   Pascal Perrineau, "Marine Le Pen: Voter pour une nouvelle extrême droite?" Pascal Perrineau et Luc Rouban, *La Solitude de l'isoloir: Les vrais enjeux de 2012* (Paris: Éditions Autrement, 2012), 25–38.

13   Sasha Issenberg, "America Exports Democracy, Just Not the Way You Think," *The New York Times*, March 14, 2014.

14   Pascal Perrineau, *Le Choix de Marianne: Pourquoi et pour qui votons nous?* (Paris: Fayard, 2012).

15   Bertrand Badie, personal interview, June 13, 2012.

DOI: 10.1057/9781137356918.0004

16 See Michael Sutton, *France and the Construction of Europe, 1944–2007* (New York: Berghahn Books, 2007).

17 The no vote on Maastricht in 1992 was 49%; in 2005 it had progressed to 55%.

18 Pascal Perrineau notes the decline of class-based voting in France along with the geographical determinants of the Right-Left division in France. These new cleavages in French politics have yet to affect the Right-Left division, and have only found clear responses in the National Front. However, the decline of historic class-based voting does not change the reality of social inequality in France. See Perrineau, *Le Choix de Marianne.*

19 Muxel, in Perrineau, *La Décision électorale*, pp. 80–86.

DOI: 10.1057/9781137356918.0004

2
The Contending Forces

Abstract: *There were ten candidates for the French presidency in 2002, five of whom were real contenders. Hollande was challenged from his left by Jean-Luc Mélenchon, a former socialist who allied with the Communists. Sarkozy was flanked on his right by the National Front, energized by the Marine Le Pen, who embarked on a new campaign of apparent moderation that masked a continued anti-system politics of racism and exclusion. A third challenge was presented by Centrist Francois Bayrou. Counting fringe candidates half the voters preferred neither Hollande nor Sarkozy, each of whom could appeal to only a quarter of the electorate. France's traditional governing parties were in crisis.*

Wall, Irwin. *France Votes: The Election of François Hollande.* New York: Palgrave Macmillan, 2014.
DOI: 10.1057/9781137356918.0005.

DOI: 10.1057/9781137356918.0005

The first round of the presidential elections demonstrated clearly that the traditional governing parties were in fact both minority parties in France. The UMP and PS were each challenged on their right and left, and both from the center. While Hollande and Sarkozy led with 29 and 27% of the vote, respectively, three challengers showed that a considerable body of opinion preferred neither of them. Marine Le Pen received an unprecedented 17.9% of the vote as leader of the right-wing National Front, and during the first ballot was engaged in her own sort of private duel with a new and dynamic figure from the Left, Jean-Luc Mélenchon, whose 11.1% total did not reflect the high-profile created by his Front de Gauche, which included the French Communist party, during the campaign. Mélenchon polled as high as 15% during the campaign, and at times appeared to overtake Le Pen's party in the contest for third place among the electorate. The enthusiastic crowds at his demonstrations recalled headier and more enthusiastic popular front years.[1]

Mélenchon had been a Socialist, trying to be the gadfly pushing the party to the Left, until he abandoned the effort in 2008, seceding with his supporters in frustration particularly with the leadership of Hollande. Hollande had never been a Marxist; there is no evidence that he read or thought about Marx, and he studiously avoided factionalism while acting as head of a party in which factions or "currents," as the French term them, were rife. Mélenchon became convinced, however, that Hollande was leading the PS toward the goal of becoming simply a "Democratic" party in the American sense; a political machine with a veneer of liberalism and perhaps some compassion, but with the primary aim of exercising power for power's sake. Mélenchon quickly steered his "Parti de Gauche," which is to be distinguished from all the other ideological currents of the French extreme Left, whether extreme Left or Trotskyist, into an alliance with the French Communist party in a new "Front de Gauche." Mélenchon was able to take about 14,000 followers with him out of the PS and into his new party. It is not clear, for all that, that Mélenchon is close to the Parti communist Français (PCF) ideologically. His philosophy does not focus on ownership of the means of production and exchange but rather the reduction of inequality, which is quite a different thing. In accomplishing that goal he would use the tax system, effecting redistribution in a way that nobody had done before.[2] But what Mélenchon did offer during the campaign was a new vitality on the Left, a sense of excitement, the ability to infuse crowds with an unalloyed enthusiasm not seen in French elections in many years.

DOI: 10.1057/9781137356918.0005

The break between Mélenchon and Hollande was personal as well as political, and there seemed little prospect of any reconciliation between them. Mélenchon's rhetorical skills managed to revitalize the Left, and although never a Communist himself, he lured much of the Communist electorate, which had abandoned the party in recent years, to come back to the fold. He brought together most or all of the groups of the extreme Left, who together garnered only about 5% of the vote in the elections of 2007, and brought them back to the respectable total of 11%, enough to be a force in French politics. His regional base of support resembled the old Communist electorate, and he also managed to bring both members of the Parti de Gauche and the PCF out into the streets for demonstrations. Hundreds of thousands responded to his call to "retake the Bastille" on the Place de la Bastille on March 18, according to reports, to the considerable annoyance of Hollande, whose own rallies failed to show the same enthusiasm. Of course Mélenchon's electorate was safely made up of Hollande voters on the second ballot; presumably Hollande had nothing to fear from them. But Hollande would have preferred to see them within the PS fold. Mélenchon's vote was unstable, moreover; his supporters tended to veer back and forth between him and Hollande on the first round, unable to decide between showing their greater radicalism by supporting him or voting "utile," usefully so to speak, to ensure against a repetition of 2002, when votes splintered between a variety of left-wing candidates caused Le Pen to emerge as the challenger to Chirac on the second ballot.

Mélenchon voters who normally supported the PS came almost entirely from those who voted no on the European constitution referendum in 2005, and after the elections Mélenchon campaigned against the pact of stability that Hollande, once in power, decided he had to sign after all. There is a dialectical relationship in play on the French political scene between Europe, the euro, and the policies of Mrs. Merkel on the one hand, and political support for Marine Le Pen and Mélenchon on the other. This to say that the dogged pursuit of austerity on the EU level is inhibiting economic growth in France, and the EU generally, contributing to the atmosphere in which more radical and extremist politics can flourish throughout Europe. In the end, Mélenchon's vote, which had threatened to eclipse that of the National Front, fell back to 11%, a disappointing result but still well ahead of where the Communists had been since their virtual collapse in the 1980s and 1990s. And added to the National Front vote it makes a solid third of the electorate hostile to

DOI: 10.1057/9781137356918.0005

the EU. There are enough voters within the ranks of the UMP and the PS who remain doubtful about or suspicious of the EU so as to insure that a majority of the electorate in France will oppose further integration, if not the Union itself.

Finally, François Bayrou's Centrist party received 9.1% of the vote, hardly negligible but still only half of what Bayrou managed in 2007 against Royal and Sarkozy. After a brief revival of the political Center in 2007, it seemed that bipolarization was likely to be the predominant characteristic of French politics; there was no longer any place for a party of the Center. Indeed it could not have been very clear to voters exactly how, in terms of economic policies, Bayrou differed from Sarkozy, whom he had supported on the second ballot in 2007, despite their sharp differences in personality. Yet, desperate for Bayrou's support on the second ballot, Royal promised to make him prime minister in 2007 if she were elected. Bayrou, of course, was a good democrat, and he was repelled by Sarkozy's demagoguery in 2012, so much so that he rallied to Hollande on the second ballot. He projected an image of rationality and compassion in addition to a concern for proper democratic procedure in his reaction to anti-immigrant politics and xenophobia, whether of the FN or of Sarkozy. But his economic message was the absolute need to balance the budget, that is to say his message was one of support for Mrs. Merkel, Europe, and austerity.

Added together, the three candidates challenging the hegemony of the two governing parties accounted for 38% of the electorate, more than either Hollande or Sarkozy could claim individually with their totals of 28.6 and 27.2%, respectively. Participation in the election was high, at 81.3%, which compares favorably with the highest figures recorded in presidential votes during the Fifth Republic, bucking the trend toward abstention. Electoral participation fell off drastically during the legislative elections, however, when on the second ballot 46% of the electorate stayed home.

There was one other candidate in the running susceptible of receiving a significant number of votes—Eva Joly, the candidate of the Ecologists. Once as high as 15% of the electorate, the ecologist movement had fallen on hard times by 2012, and despite Joly's presence on the ballot concerns for the environment were not high on the agenda or much mentioned during the campaign. The Socialists, before the campaign, had thought it in their interest to secure the support of the Ecologists, and to have their party as part of the governing majority. Despite Joly's decision to

DOI: 10.1057/9781137356918.0005

run as an independent candidate against Hollande on the first ballot of the presidential race, 60 electoral districts were reserved for Ecologists to run as candidates of a united Left in the legislative elections, allowing the party to emerge with 19 seats in the National Assembly, and Hollande appointed two Ecologists as Ministers in his first government. The major concern of the PS, the Ecologists, and the electorate was the dependence of France on nuclear power as the source of electricity. Currently nuclear plants provide France with 75% of its electricity needs. A legacy of de Gaulle's quest for economic power and prestige, France's aging nuclear plants today seem rather menacing in the wake of Fukushima although France is unlikely to experience a quake of similar magnitude or a tsunami. Hollande was willing to move toward reducing France's reliance on nuclear energy, targeting a reduction to 50% of electricity needs produced by nuclear power by the end of his first term, and eventually closing an aging nuclear plant at Fessenheim, in Alsace, near the German and Swiss borders. There is further controversy over a "new generation" nuclear plant in Normandy at Flamanville, located on the Contentin peninsula not far from Cherbourg, which is in an area susceptible to flooding. Technical problems with its construction have led to huge cost overruns. The French public appears generally to support the Socialist-Ecologist goal of reducing the nation's reliance on nuclear power to 50%. Joly is a judge known for fighting corruption in France; she is of Norwegian background, speaks French with a heavy accent, and turned out to be an unprepossessing candidate. Nor did she present a coherent program of government aside from environmental concerns. She received only 2.3% of the vote.

There were four more candidates on the first ballot in 2012. It is fairly easy to qualify for the ballot in France—one only needs to garner the requisite number of signatures from local officials, many of whom are frequently quite willing to support dissident candidates. Philippe Poutou ran as the candidate of the New Anti-Capitalist Party, a formation that appeared to have some promise as a radical Left group when headed by the relatively popular Olivier Besancenot, who received 4.25% of the vote in the 2002 elections. Besancenot managed to receive over 4% of the vote again on the first ballot in 2007, but he declined to run again in 2012, and under Poutou his movement appears to have fallen apart. Nathalie Arthaud represented Lutte Ouvrière (Workers' Struggle), a Trotskyist group that also once had some luster. But her candidacy, like that of Poutou, seems to have been swamped by the appearance on the scene of

DOI: 10.1057/9781137356918.0005

Mélenchon, who monopolized the space for a more radical Left than the PS. Nicolas Dupont-Aignan ran as an independent conservative opposed to the euro in the name of national sovereignty, and Jacques Cheminade ran as a kind of French Libertarian on a platform like that of Lyndon Larouche in the United States.

The term "extremism" needs clarification in the French context. It is common for analysts to lump together the alleged extremism of Le Pen and Mélenchon. But if there is or was a national consensus among the other parties on Le Pen's "extremism," there is none on the alleged extremism of Mélenchon. The Front de Gauche poses no threat to the Republic or human rights; the Front National arguably does, even after taking into account its move toward moderation under Marine Le Pen. The PS was ready to include the Front de Gauche in its governing majority if necessary, and the Front de Gauche supported the Socialists on the second ballot. The National Front's democratic credentials remained suspect, however, and it arguably advocates discrimination against racial minorities. It is true that Marine Le Pen's greater popularity than that of her father reflects her having toned down if not forsaken some of his more extreme positions, in particular his anti-Semitism and Holocaust denial. She has also adopted some Republican allusions in her speeches and even endorsed the historic revolutionary *Declaration of the Rights of Man and Citizen*. During the campaign President Sarkozy himself, in appealing to Le Pen voters on the second ballot, endorsed her "republicanism."[3] Still, the party remains very much an "anti-system" party, its primary goals remaining exclusion of the other and "security" (crime and delinquency are associated with the minority populations in France). The supporters of the National Front in their vast majority agree with the proposition that there are "too many immigrants in France." Marine Le Pen has also recast the National Front to give it a social, if not leftist dimension. She is quietly building a French variant of national-socialism although a far cry from the Nazi variety.[4]

The National Front nevertheless remains the primary destabilizing element of the French political scene today, and it seemed to be growing further after the elections as the initial enthusiasm for Hollande waned. To understand its emergence we must again step back to review some recent French history.

The National Front has already become the longest enduring of France's historic right-wing political parties. Its predecessors in the postwar period were the Poujadist movement, which gained 12% of the vote in the

DOI: 10.1057/9781137356918.0005

elections of 1956, and the die-hard proponents of *Algérie Française*, headed by Tixier-Vignancour, who challenged de Gaulle for reelection in 1965, but managed a mere 5.2% of the vote. The Poujade movement dissipated in the rally around de Gaulle of the French Right in 1958. The National Front differs from the Poujadistes: Pierre Poujade was a representative of a movement of small businessmen, self-employed artisans, and farmers threatened by modernization whose extremist nationalism found expression in what was basically an anti-tax movement. The National Front is very much an urban movement, even if its leader, Jean-Marie Le Pen, first appeared on the political scene as a Poujadist deputy in the National Assembly, where he distinguished himself by a virulent campaign in favor of keeping Algeria French and a personal anti-Semitic attack on the former (Jewish) prime minister of the era, Pierre Mendès France.

The radical Right in France had declined to less than 1% estimated support when Le Pen undertook to reorganize it into the National Front in October 1972. The National Front was launched by a fascist group, Ordre Nouveau, whose members sought an electoral arm to supplement their pro-Nazi propaganda and paramilitary style politics of confrontation with the extreme Left. They invited Jean-Marie Le Pen, who combined a personable political style with his right-wing politics, to be their public voice. Le Pen performed skillfully in that capacity and he soon took over the National Front; he attracted to it an amalgam of the classic French Right, including remnants of the Vichy regime, Poujadism, and Algerian settlers who settled in France after Algerian independence in 1962, and he provided a certain charismatic leadership, while de-emphasizing the politics of confrontation and elevating the importance of electoral politics. The trick was in doing so while maintaining the characteristics of the FN as an "anti-system" party.

Le Pen endowed the National Front with a tight, authoritarian organization but it remained a fringe group through the 1970s, its participation in elections gaining it little more than 1% of the vote, and in the 1981 elections Le Pen failed to garner the 500 signatures of local officials necessary to launch his candidacy for president. The long-term depression that began the 1970s and the failure of the Socialist government headed by President François Mitterrand to address it in the 1980s provided the conjuncture for the electoral breakthrough of the National Front.

The Mitterrand government was almost revolutionary in the massive changes it initially introduced in 1981 after its election victory. A large segment of the economy was nationalized, wages and pensions were

DOI: 10.1057/9781137356918.0005

raised in an effort to stimulate the economy according to Keynesian doctrine, and a massive program of political decentralization was begun. In 1983, however, under budgetary pressure and European warnings, Mitterrand backtracked on many of his reforms and imposed a policy of "rigor" or austerity designed to keep budgetary expenses in balance. The 1980s elsewhere were the years of a new conservatism in Europe under the leadership of Ronald Reagan in the United States and Margaret Thatcher in Great Britain. Their ideological hegemony was not simply a victory of "supply-side" economics over Keynesian nostrums that had previously been popular; it was rather the emergence of a new and powerful consensus on neo-liberal capitalism inspired by the economic philosophy of Friedrich von Hayek, and it involved seeking to reduce the power of labor unions and retrenching or reversing directions in the growth of the welfare state. Having discovered that "socialism in one country" was out of the question in France without a severe break with the growing movement toward European unity, Mitterrand turned from social reform toward European unity as the hallmark of his presidency, reacting to the conservative political climate that prevailed around him. The collapse of communism was a kind of coda to the preceding triumph of neo-liberal capitalism, and it also led to a revolution in the European power relationship as Germany became unified, growing from a nation roughly equal in size to France (about 60 million) into a new powerhouse of over 80 million. The response of Mitterrand was to try and tie Germany that much more closely to the European project; indeed the price of his consent to German unification was the German commitment to further steps toward European unity, and in particular a common European currency. These new steps were embodied in the Maastricht Treaty of 1992.

It was a great shock when the Maastricht Treaty, binding a unified Germany to Europe in the project for a European currency, came near to being rejected in a referendum called by Mitterrand in 1992. And as the decade progressed, Left disillusionment seemed to lead to progress for the National Front as political scientists diagnosed a growing crisis in the French body politic characterized by the alienation of "civil society," a term very much in vogue since the collapse of communism in 1989–1991, from the political class. It has frequently been observed that the French political class is a kind of hermetically closed elite. Many are products of the so-called Grandes Ecoles, the elite schools that get superior treatment to the universities in terms of funds and learning conditions and which

DOI: 10.1057/9781137356918.0005

were historically available only to the top few of the upper bourgeoisie by competitive examination. To be sure, entrance to these schools has been expanded in recent years, but the competitive examinations still reserve seats for an advantaged elite, and within these the Ecole Nationale d'Administration, the elite of the elite, produces most of the top politicians, party leaders, and presidents who form a kind of meritocracy. Jacques Chirac, Lionel Jospin, Ségolène Royal, and François Hollande are among its graduates. Hermetically sealed, the French political class has also become corrupt, and scandals rock the French body politic with great regularity. Former presidents Chirac and Sarkozy both left political office under a cloud with the possibility of subsequent indictment by the judiciary hanging over them. The alienation of the public from the political class has become manifest in the growing abstention rate in national elections and the corresponding rise of the right-wing populist party, the National Front.

The National Front is further fueled by the euro crisis; Hollande is between a rock and a hard place, squeezed by the contrary but mutually reinforcing politics of two powerful women, Marine Le Pen and Angela Merkel. The euro did not yet exist in 1983, but Mitterrand's sudden turn to the Right provided the climate for the breakthrough of the National Front, which came in the small city (population, 30,000) of Dreux in 1983, where a political entrepreneur, Jean-Pierre Stirbois, garnered 16% of the vote in a municipal by-election and then fused his list with the Gaullist and Centrist Right to take control of the city administration.[5] It bears noting that in 1983 Mitterrand definitively abandoned the Left politics he had been pursuing since his dramatic victory in the 1981 elections. From that point on Mitterrand became a strong proponent of Europe and the Franco-German partnership. Not accidentally, similar strong FN showings followed in other by-elections, and then the FN managed 10% of the vote in the elections to the European parliament of 1984, and 11% in the legislative elections of 1986. The Socialist government of François Mitterrand introduced proportional representation in the election of 1986, which gave the party further prominence and visibility as 35 FN deputies took their seats in the newly elected National Assembly that anyway had a right-wing majority and no need of FN support.

The FN drew its strength from the onset of the postwar depression in the 1970s and the dramatic failure of the left-wing government of Mitterrand, despite its extensive nationalization of the French economy, to do much about the resulting unemployment in the 1980s. The 1980s

DOI: 10.1057/9781137356918.0005

were years of right-wing radicalization and political polarization almost everywhere in the west, and the parallel decline of Communism and Catholicism, previously important determinants of voting behavior in France during that period, further fueled a nationalist resurgence. The National Front fed on a mood of pessimism and a sense of cultural and economic decline in France that found further expression in a falling birthrate. Although the French birthrate is among the highest of the European countries, it is still not much above replacement level, and the immigrant birth level is higher than that of the longer-resident French. Le Pen initially attacked viciously the law permitting abortion in the 1970s, which incidentally had been introduced by a Jewish woman politician of the era, Simone Veil, and he called for a strong policy of government encouragement of a high birthrate.[6] But the most ingenious of Le Pen's innovations was the idea of tying the high rate of unemployment in France to the number of immigrants in the country: one million unemployed, went the slogan, were the consequence of one million immigrants too many in France who took jobs away from the French. Immigrants were also held by the FN to be responsible for growing crime and personal insecurity in France, and the party campaigned for increased policing, a strong and repressive state, and vigorous implementation of the death penalty, which the Mitterrand government was about to abolish.[7] The FN's xenophobic pro-French ideology expressed itself in the demand for a strong policy of "national preference" for native Frenchmen and Frenchwomen over foreigners in jobs and education, in effect a euphemism for blatant discrimination.[8]

There is great irony in Le Pen's clever use of the immigration issue to put the National Front at the forefront of French politics. France has been a country of immigrants since the 19th century. Immigration has in fact historically been necessary to compensate for the country's low birthrate. There have been several distinct waves of immigration; largely Belgian and Italian before the First World War, and predominately Polish and East European between the wars. Poles and Southern East Europeans were openly recruited by a semi-public French immigration agency to work in the French coal and iron mines. After the Second World War the French birthrate turned upward, but there was still barely enough labor to fuel the postwar boom as France became a consumer economy. Spanish and Portuguese workers flocked to France in the 1950s and 1960s. Algeria had always been regarded legally as part of France, and its Muslim residents began a massive immigration to France in

DOI: 10.1057/9781137356918.0005

search of employment as well. During the Algerian war, 1954–1962, their numbers increased dramatically; ironically they came to France to work to replace the half million young Frenchmen who were conscripted to fight the rebels in their own country as France struggled mightily in the vain hope of maintaining the fiction that Algeria was not a colony but French territory. After the Algerian war ended in 1962 France achieved a growth rate of 8% per annum, and Algerians continued to augment the French labor force, alongside many Tunisians and Moroccans. North Africans are the largest contingent of French Muslim immigration, but large numbers of black Africans from France's former colonies became part of the French labor force in those years as well. The Portuguese were the largest single bloc of immigrants until the 1990s, however.

The French ceased importing labor in 1974 and immigration was reduced dramatically that year. The Conseil d'Etat, which acts as France's highest court for administrative justice, ruled that France must continue to accept immigrants for purposes of family reunion, and some thousands of immigrants have entered France legally since then under that rubric.[9] But the inflow averaged between 50,000 and 100,000 per year from 2000 until 2008, and it has been somewhat higher since then (although a constant percentage normed to the population), its influence exaggerated by a net outflow of native French seeking economic opportunity abroad. The outflow of native French became an issue during the campaign and Hollande has been asked questions about how he might stop it at news conferences since being elected. But the total number of "immigrants" in the strict sense of the word has actually been in decline since the National Front began its agitation on the issue, and the balance of positive immigration into France, influx minus outflow, has declined to about 54,000 per year from 2010 through 2012. Moreover, the strictly speaking immigrant generation lessens each year, leaving more and more naturally born French Muslim citizens in its wake. No matter: the FN expanded the term "immigré" to mean Muslim generally, and it added its traditional anti-Semitism to the mix as well. There are an estimated 5–6 million Muslims in France today of a total population of 65 million, of whom 2 million actually practice the religion. Although less than 10% of the population, they account for near 30% of the yearly births, helping to make the French birthrate, along with that of Ireland, the highest in the European Union.

The politicization of the immigration issue left the traditional parties in a bind, coming after the fact as it were. Both governing parties have

DOI: 10.1057/9781137356918.0005

been reduced to a posture of becoming "tough" on the issue in order to compete with the FN for votes. Laws have been passed to make expulsions of illegals easier, but their numbers have never been high to begin with. There are no longer controls on the French frontiers with other EU countries, since under the Schengen agreement and EU regulations goods and peoples of the EU cross frontiers easily. Control of illegal immigration to the EU is governed in terms of human rights under the Schengen agreement, and implemented by the member states, but more directly concerns Italy, Greece, and Spain, all of which more directly neighbor North Africa and the Middle East than France. These nations have reached a crisis point in trying to stem the number of illegal entries, and the EU has created a new agency, Frontex, to deal in common with the external immigration flow. The FN has made good use of an existing problem, probably generational, but unlikely to go away in the short run, or the long run either as anti-immigrant prejudice is transformed into overt racial prejudice tout court. But its electoral salience is lessened, if not neutralized, by the Muslim vote, which appears to lean overwhelmingly Left; and Hollande's espousal of giving immigrants who are long-term legal residents in France the right to vote in local elections has no doubt helped him with Muslim voters. A recent study by Jerome Fourquet of IFOP put the Muslim vote for Hollande at 86% in the recent election. Muslims are only 5% of the French electorate, however, because they do not vote in the same percentages as the French, and as mentioned earlier, their electoral punch is lessened by their high concentration in specific areas. But the overwhelming margin in favor of Hollande in the Muslim community accounts for a good part of his margin of victory in 2012.[10]

But on the other hand Sarkozy probably won over just as many anti-Muslim voters with his blatant anti-immigrant appeals. In the voting for the National Assembly, moreover, the influence of individual electoral districts of high immigration and corresponding Muslim voters, moreover, seems to be neutralized. High levels of immigrant concentration in France seem to be concentrated in suburban departments and often in electoral districts that anyway vote for the Right. And where immigrants themselves vote in their majority for the Left, there seems to be a counter-effect in that white areas in proximity to large concentrations of immigrants are drawn to vote for the National Front. Immigrant concentrations in Left-voting districts simply add to the scale of the Left's victory. The total effect on individual districts, however, runs in favor of the extreme Right, especially as the FN has developed its appeal

DOI: 10.1057/9781137356918.0005

to former Communist voters. The complexity of the influence of the immigrant presence, whether in districts leaning to the Right or the Left, has meant that the traditional political parties do not find it to their advantage to field minority candidates either.

Nor is there a "Jewish vote" in France per se; both parties do field Jewish candidates for office but without consideration of any ethnic vote or the number of Jews in the population. Estimates of the number of French Jews have varied between 500,000 and 700,000 in recent years, but conservative estimates putting the real number in the range of 500,000 now seem in favor. In public opinion polls over the years only 0.7% of the French self-identify as Jews. However in the current political climate many are reluctant to so identify publicly. In reaction to Gaulle's shift to an anti-Israel foreign policy in the 1960s, which was continued by his successors in the 1970s, Jews voted heavily for François Mitterrand in 1981. Mitterrand in particular made much of his presumed ties of friendship to Israeli Labor politicians. However, since the second Intifada of 2000–2001 and the consequent resurgence of anti-Semitism in France, the Jewish vote has shifted toward the Right. Sarkozy, who boasts some Jewish ethnicity, led France back into NATO and toward a more balanced if not pro-Israel foreign policy after 2007. While there are no statistics on the Jewish vote in France to the extent that it exists, Jérome Fourquet, who has done several studies of the issue, notes an evolution among Jews toward the political Right since the turn of the 21st century, and Sarkozy has known how to appeal to them. According to some estimates Sarkozy got 64% of the Jewish vote in 2012, interestingly about the same percentage he garnered among practicing Catholics in France.[11] Among French Jews resident in Israel, Sarkozy won overwhelmingly.[12]

Le Pen managed to incorporate the newest campaigning techniques into the National Front's appeal. His campaign posters projected his personality in "presidential" style, conservatively dressed, hair coiffed, and doctored photographs managing to project a youthful but mature image under a head of grey hair (he was born in 1928, and thus was in his fifties at the time of the FN's electoral breakthrough). Le Pen skillfully managed to attract both a petty bourgeoisie in the cities threatened by big business, modernization, and globalization, and a declining industrial working class that fell victim to the same forces as France began its experience of post-industrialization and transition to a service economy common to the industrial powers of the West. The National Front supporters reflect the typology of the right-wing voters who rallied to

DOI: 10.1057/9781137356918.0005

the support of fascist parties during the interwar period: they are very much a declining middle class threatened by modernization, the losers in the process of globalization as fascism in the 1930s represented the losers in industrialization. Le Pen's electoral base at once reflected the nationalist enclaves of the South of France, the Mediterranean littoral of Marseilles, Nice, Toulon, where the FN was able to win by itself in several cities (Orange, Marignane), and the former Communist departments of the Nord and Pas-de-Calais.[13] The East of France, in particular Alsace-Lorraine, further provided a bastion of support. The National Front deputies, meanwhile, drew upon an upper bourgeoisie of bureaucrats, businessmen, and professionals. It was at once very much a "catch-all party" yet united by an anti-system mood reflecting a strange paradox; it attracted an electorate of the extreme Right and joined it to the historic bastions of the extreme Left. These characteristics of FN voters were still evident in the 2012 elections: FN voters were still 54% male, 28% under age 35, 32% employés (non-industrial salaried workers), 31% working class, 72% among the least educated, and 39% drawn from those workers earning under 2,000 euros per month.[14]

The French seemed wedded to the hybrid institutions of the Fifth Republic which pretend to be both presidential and parliamentary; yet they began in the 1980s to express growing disillusionment with the political class that showed both of the traditional governing parties, the Gaullist-Centrist coalition and the PS with its Communist and diverse left-wing allies, to be declining in strength. The National Front filled this newly created void by bespeaking an angry form of anti-system populism that is both xenophobic and racist, and its voters were only minimally bothered by the penchant of Le Pen to show the vulgar prejudices of a once-discredited wartime Right; he expressed sympathy for holocaust denial, for example, and while admitting the existence of gas chambers during the Second World War he dismissed them as a "detail."[15] In 2005, to the embarrassment of his daughter who was trying to humanize the FN's image, he said that the German occupation of France during the Second World War had not been particularly "inhumane." If these statements turned many potential supporters away, Le Pen's blanket condemnation of the existing political parties of the time into a corrupt "gang of four," (Gaullist RPR, Centrist UDF, Socialist PS, and Communist PCF), emphasizing the FN as the virtuous "outsider," became a further powerful element of attraction.

Statistics do show a preponderance of specific characteristics of FN voters and militants. Until the 2012 elections they were still predominately

DOI: 10.1057/9781137356918.0005

male and young; the party's greatest appeal was among voters aged 18–30. While most openly identified with the political Right, as many expressed disgust with both supposed ends of the political continuum, Right and Left. These voters hoped to transcend traditional politics and bring in a new kind of social system, a "third way" between capitalism and socialism. Nonna Mayer divides FN supporters into "Droitistes" and "Ninistes," that is to say those who regard themselves as on the extreme Right of the political spectrum and those who claim to be neither Right nor Left.[16] All FN voters are populist and anti-elitist, however: Le Pen framed his appeal to the disinherited, "*Vous, les petits gens, les sans grade, les exclus...*" Most FN voters have less education and fewer of them have attained the Bac; in general, the higher the level of one's education the less is the attraction to FN politics.[17] They believe in conspiracies and crave an authoritarian state that can restore law and order.

On two occasions in the FN's recent past it seemed that the party had crested in support and might be headed for a future of decline if not disappearance. In 1998 Le Pen faced a challenge to his leadership from a former lieutenant Bruno Mégret. Mégret advocated a policy of alliance and mutual support in run-off elections with the traditional Right, the Gaullist and Centrist parties, which would have had as a natural corollary the entry of FN politicians into conservative government coalitions to share political power. Le Pen was violently opposed to this policy. Politically his sympathies were with the so-called ninistes, those who saw no difference between the two political groups that governed France, conservative or socialist. He parroted the Communist party on this question, quoting the one-time revered Communist leader Jacques Duclos who had once attacked the rival candidates in the 1969 presidential elections as "bonnet blanc" versus "blanc bonnet." More seriously he feared falling victim to the Communist party's recent fate: François Mitterrand took the Communists into his coalition government in 1981 with the intended effect of smothering them as an independent political force while stealing away their political support. The subsequent decline in the PCF vote showed that he was eminently successful. Le Pen was afraid that the UMP might do the same to his movement if he allied with it. Ironically much of the support of disaffected Communists would seem to have been inherited by Le Pen, however, rather than the PS.

The dispute with Le Pen over tactics led Mégret to break away from the FN to form his own party. At first it seemed he might be able to mount a serious challenge to Le Pen but that was to lose sight of the latter's

DOI: 10.1057/9781137356918.0005

apparent charisma. Much of the FN's support was tied up with Le Pen's personality. This became apparent with the landmark elections of 2002. Following his lackluster performance as prime minister in a government of "cohabitation" under President Chirac in the late 1990s, Lionel Jospin became the Socialist party's standard bearer in the presidential elections of 2002. Disillusionment with Jospin led to the appearance of a wide variety of left-wing challengers on the first ballot of the election with various ecologists, dissident socialists, and even two relatively strong Trotskyist parties emerging to challenge Jospin along with the traditional Communist party and other groups of the extreme Left. The result was stunning: Jospin's total vote on the second ballot was 16.18% as opposed to 19% for President Chirac and 16.84% on the first ballot for Jean-Marie Le Pen. Despite losing over 2% of his vote to Brunot Mégret, Le Pen emerged as the sole challenger to Chirac on the second ballot. The result came as a great shock to the French electorate, and public opinion from all parties rallied to Chirac's support on the second ballot.

Consequently Chirac emerged as the overwhelming victor with 82.21% of the vote to Le Pen's 17.79%. On one level Le Pen's showing could be interpreted as a demonstration of the strong antipathy the FN generated in France as a threat to democratic values. Le Pen had barely increased his total on the second ballot, not even fully recuperating the portion of the vote that had gone to his right-wing challenger, Mégret, in the first round (2.34%). But on a more ominous level it seemed that despite its relatively strong defeat the National Front was well on its way to becoming the second major political force in France.

This was to reason without taking into account the FN's second major challenge, the new dynamic face of the Gaullist RPR, Nicolas Sarkozy. Sarkozy readily recognized the ability of the FN to draw off right-wing voters from France's conservative parties, and he took seriously Le Pen's ambition to replace the RPR and its Center allies as the dominant political force on the French political Right. He consequently adopted a nationalist tone, making his own the FN's concern with French affirmation of national identity, and as France's minister of the interior, made it clear that he was conscious of that position as the historic vantage point that Clemenceau once termed it: he was the head cop of France. Sarkozy undertook to deal with the challenge to "law and order" presented by the situation in France's immigrant suburbs, where high rates of youth unemployment led to unrest, protests, burnings of automobiles, and regular clashes with the police. Promising a strong hand in dealing with

DOI: 10.1057/9781137356918.0005

immigrants appeared to be the way to build a strong political base at the expense of Le Pen and for Sarkozy it was. Surviving even a challenge to Jacques Chirac from within the RPR, Sarkozy emerged as the head of the party and its presidential candidate in the elections of 2007. He faced a new personality on the Left in Ségolène Royal, the first woman to run for the presidency of France, whom he bested by in fact taking back for the traditional French Right a good part of Le Pen's electorate. Showing almost unprecedented popularity for a right-wing candidate, excepting the legendary founder of the Fifth Republic, Charles de Gaulle, Sarkozy received over 32% of the votes on the first ballot in 2007, coming in well ahead of Royal, who managed, however, to bring the PS back to a respectable figure, 25%. But if Sarkozy had defeated Royal, however, he had won an even more decisive victory over Le Pen, whose party he had reduced to size. Appearing aged and tired Le Pen got a mere 10.44% of the vote on the first ballot in 2007. With an invigorated conservatism in power it seemed once again reasonable to draw the conclusion that the FN was now definitively on the way to being marginalized as a major political force in France.

It fell to Le Pen's daughter Marine to bring the FN back to its previous position of major player, if not kingmaker, of French politics by 2012. Marine Le Pen appeared on the scene in 2002, taking charge of the party's youth group with the moniker Génération Le Pen. Her ascension marked a certain tightening of control and concern for personal loyalty on the part of her father: he not only supported her advancement but put his two sons-in-law, Samuel Maréchal and Philippe Olivier, in positions of authority as well. After the 2007 elections Marine appeared as responsible for major party concerns, education, communications, and propaganda, while holding the shared title of executive vice president with long-time party stalwart Bruno Gollisch. Gollisch presented her competition only for party leadership, but his campaign was constrained by his personal loyalty to her father. Nor could he hope to compete with her obvious strength as the party's unofficial spokesperson to the media: she showed exceptional skills, especially on television, her personality doing more than anything she said to show, as some sarcastically put it, "fascism with a human face." Marine set out to turn the party in a new direction with the policy known as "dédiabolisation," by which she meant shedding its notorious (devilish) image and making it appear, within limits, a "normal" political party like others. She specifically repudiated anti-Semitism and holocaust denial. Her new line endorsed

DOI: 10.1057/9781137356918.0005

the values of the Republic, in particular the declaration of the rights of man, and she rediscovered *laicité*, perceiving that anti-clericalism could be used as a powerful weapon against Islam. The National Front also now endorses the full range of social legislation of the French welfare state and condemns untrammeled capitalism. Both liberal capitalism and the assault on the French welfare state are attributed to the reactionary politics of the European Union. Repudiating suggestions of racism, a new euphemistic language recast "national preference" as national "solidarity" while members of racial minorities were featured mouthing the party line on posters and television ads. The message now seemed to be that national minorities were fine so long as they assimilated to the values and behavior and cultural practices of the French majority. The party changed its position on divorce, abortion, and homosexuality, accepting them all. After Hollande's election Marine Le Pen declined to become part of the popular, largely Catholic protest against gay marriage.[18]

Marine Le Pen set herself four goals in the elections of 2012, all of which she achieved brilliantly. Thought previously to be in decline, the FN reestablished itself ominously on the French political scene. Her successes were to outdo the vote totals of her father, to impose the rhetoric of predilection and exclusion on the national campaign debate, confer upon the FN a new moderate image, and by defeating President Sarkozy, mount a challenge to the traditional Right as the voice of opposition to the newly consecrated governing Socialist party.[19] Whether the party's quest for normalization was anything more than cosmetic, however, remained to be seen. Hers remained an anti-system party even if she now accepts the Republic; she could not completely exorcise the devil because the devil in the FN was what so many of her followers liked. During the elections the FN remained an "anti-system" party, the "system" meaning the political domination of what she terms the "UMPS." The FN continued to link immigration, insecurity, and unemployment, and it condemned both government parties for failing to deal with them. While trying to shed the FN of its image of disrepute Marine Le Pen diabolized the EU in turn as that "monstre européiste," referred to the IMF, European Bank, and European Union as a "three-headed monster," and condemned globalization as "*identicide*." The FN still wanted a strong state and repressive apparatus crowned by the death penalty. It wanted to legalize discrimination in the form of national preference and expel unspecified numbers of immigrants. It was not clear

DOI: 10.1057/9781137356918.0005

whether once in power, the FN would govern democratically. It did not shed its identity as a party of the extreme Right.

There was much expression of anguish at Marine Le Pen's vote total in 2012, but it was not exactly an all-time high for the FN in terms of percentage of the vote. In the 2002 elections Jean-Marie Le Pen received 16.86% on the first ballot, but the split in the FN lost him another 2.34% siphoned off by Bruno Mégret. If one adds these together one gets 19.2%, considerably more than Marine Le Pen's 17.9% in 2012. It is also worth noting that having emerged as the leading opposition candidate to Jacques Chirac in 2002, Jean-Marie Le Pen failed to draw any additional votes to himself on the second ballot. His slightly less than 17% total indicated that he did not even get the votes of half the dissenting Mégret supporters.[20]

Even more interesting were the intentions of FN voters on the second ballot of the 2012 elections. Marine Le Pen called upon them to abstain, but only 21% of them apparently heeded her appeal. Even more interesting, only 48% of the remainder said they would vote for Sarkozy, despite his blatant appeal to them to support him and his evocation of anti-immigrant themes to do so. Instead, 31% expressed their intention to vote for François Hollande.[21] This raises interesting questions about the Le Pen vote. It is fluid; many more people have voted for the FN one or more times, some estimates as high as 28%, but many of them drift back to the more established parties. On the second ballot they abandon the FN, heeding injunctions to "vote utile," meaning make their vote count by casting it for a candidate likely to win. And enough of them return to the Left, in this case giving Hollande a lift of 5% on the second ballot, more than enough to provide his margin of victory over Sarkozy.

This raises questions about the FN vote analogous to the questions once raised about the Communist party which regularly garnered more than 20% of the vote during the Fourth Republic and the early years of the Fifth Republic. The noted political scientist Georges Lavau then interpreted the Communist vote as "tribunitary," voters in his view voting Communist to express their protest or unhappiness at the choice as existing but without expectation or even desire that the PCF actually win or take power. As the Communists once gave voice to protests over inequality, the FN gives voice to complaints about the excesses of Europeanization and the alleged overly favorable treatment of immigrants in France and lax external policies permitting too many new ones to come. The vote is only partially an actual vote for the party to come to

DOI: 10.1057/9781137356918.0005

power; it is rather a message to the governing parties of the unhappiness at the existing state of affairs they presumably need to remedy. The caveat here, however, is that as the politics of austerity continue in Europe and are administered in France by President Hollande, support for the FN continues to grow, while loyalty among FN voters, past supporters voting FN again, increases as well.

Putting aside the issue of extremism, it is worthwhile to look more closely at the three dissident movements of the 2012 campaign, those of Le Pen, Mélenchon, and Bayrou. Bayrou in contrast to the firebrand politics of Le Pen and Mélenchon got a kind of grudging admiration from the press for his rationalism and efforts to overcome partisanship in a futile search for compromise in the national interest. But all three challengers of the established parties, Le Pen, Bayrou, and Mélenchon, represented something fundamental and otherwise lacking in French politics. There is or should not be anything regarded as extreme in Mélenchon's insistence on the necessity for basic, structural economic change in the direction of greater equality within France and the emancipation of the economy from the stranglehold of external financiers and bankers. Nor is there necessarily something wrong in the Lepeniste insistence on security and regulation of France's immigration process, which often seems out of control not only in France but in all of Europe. The "extremism" of both Mélenchon and Le Pen lies in the means of expression of their messages rather than the content, and their hysterical fear if not hatred of each other. Indeed, one can imagine, as Jean-Francois Kahn does in a short polemic titled *La Catastrophe du 6 Mai 2012*, a perfect world in which the core rational element in the demands of both might find formulation in Bayrou's call for a sensible, pragmatic approach to politics.[22] Bayrou tried to offer a way out of the tactical war for power conducted by the UMP and the PS, who were in his view caught up in a mutual and perhaps destructive impasse over the means of achieving their own power, which they too often confused with the public good. But theirs was not a perfect world, and the messages of Mélenchon, Le Pen, and Bayrou seemed as if they were made for cacophony rather than harmony.

The election of 2012 was of necessity a referendum on Sarkozy's presidency. Nicolas Sarkozy represented an anomaly among French presidents, a characteristic that Hollande seized upon in promising to restore to the nation a "normal" presidency. The 2007 election of Sarkozy was termed by him a vote of "rupture," a break with the status quo. This is all the more remarkable in that it came on the heels of two successive terms

DOI: 10.1057/9781137356918.0005

of the conservative presidency of Jacques Chirac, lasting twelve years (a reform of 2002 reduced the terms of French presidents to five from seven years). The nation was tired of Chirac, who was deeply unpopular, and ready for a change; and the Left had won control of most of the regions of France in local elections. It seemed a golden opportunity for the Socialist Party to come to power, all the more so with the fresh candidacy of Ségolène Royal, the first woman to run for the presidency of France at the head of one of the traditional governing parties.

Sarkozy appeared a fresh and unusual challenger for the presidency, however, despite having made his career under Chirac, and he seized the mantle of challenger for himself, running against the legacy of Chirac, under whom he had served both as minister of the interior and minister of finance, two of the most powerful cabinet posts. In those posts he projected an image of youth and dynamism against the backdrop of the aging President Chirac; as an activist minister he won great personal popularity. This was all the more remarkable given his stark differences from the men who had traditionally governed France, at least since the direct election of presidents since the 1960s. His name, Sarkozy, was Hungarian, reflecting the origins of his father, who was an immigrant in France when Sarkozy was born. His mother was French, but herself the daughter of a French mother and an immigrant Jew from Greek Salonika. Sarkozy's ethnicity was reflected in his appearance, short of stature, curly hair, somewhat swarthy complexion, he was a mixture of Hungarian, Greek-Jewish, and French forebearers, a multi-ethnic person for the first time contesting the presidency in a nation that unlike the rest of Europe has been a country of immigrants rather than the reverse, but has previously always chosen its presidents from "la France profonde," the depths of native Frenchmen. Englishmen, Germans, Italians, all varieties of East Europeans, and Russians have all peopled France as they have the United States. The French are conspicuous in America by their relative absence. They have been too busy absorbing Italians, Spaniards, Portuguese, Poles, Russians, and Jews themselves.

Sarkozy tried for diversity in his cabinet, appointing a number of women and ethnic minorities to major posts, notably Rachida Dati, of Moroccan and Algerian parentage, as minister of justice, and he also tried for a broad-based and somewhat ecumenical government by appointing Bernard Kouchner, a Socialist, the founder of "Doctors Without Borders," as minister of foreign affairs. His government got off to a terrible start, however, when he celebrated his election victory at Fouquet,

DOI: 10.1057/9781137356918.0005

the glitziest of Paris restaurants, and took a cruise on a luxury yacht lent him by one of his many wealthy friends. Sarkozy took a cavalier attitude toward money; he called for a political Right that was "décomplexée," in a word, proud to be upper bourgeois and unapologetic about showing its wealth, and he accompanied his own overt taste for luxury with a parallel quest for celebrity. He quickly won the moniker of "president bling-bling." He also seemed hyperactive, very much a hands-on president who sought personal control and initial flashy innovation in every aspect of executive bureaucracy, visiting each ministry or government department for a day and leaving seemingly innovative directives that were left without follow-up; president bling-bling also became known as the "hyper-president." He also demonstrated exactly how atypical he could be as a French president when he dressed down a critic in public with the insulting phrase "caisse-toi pauvre con," politely translated as "get lost, loser," but vulgar enough to be shocking and undignified, un-presidential to say the least, enough to turn away critics who were willing to tolerate a president seen jogging in shorts and T-shirt but not one who was a habitué of gutter language.

Sarkozy put campaign promises into legislation with his unpopular "fiscal shield," which protected the rich from any combination of taxes amounting to more than 50% of income, and he appeared to make it even clearer in whose interest he governed by raising the French retirement date for specific categories of workers from age 60 to 62.[23] Pension reform was widely thought to be necessary in France and elsewhere, of course. Nor among parties of the European Right should Sarkozy's UMP be considered a particularly reactionary example. The moderate Right has had four incarnations in France since the founding of the Fifth Republic by de Gaulle in 1958 and the original Gaullist party has been central to all of them. The Gaullists themselves were flanked by a traditional and centrist Christian-Democratic group (occasionally in a separate but allied party) on one side and a liberal-free market capitalist strain on the other, inspired to some degree by Reaganite-Thatcherist supply-side nostrums dating from the decade of the 1980s.[24] As secretary-general of a newly founded UMP (dating from the aftermath of the election debacle of 2002, when Chirac defeated Le Pen on the second ballot by 82% to 18%) Sarkozy built it into a well-oiled political and electoral machine. The moniker "Union of the Popular Movement" deliberately refused to label the party, emphasizing instead its catch-all quality. Economically conservative, it remains politically and socially in some respects liberal in the American sense of the term. It does not seek to dismantle the French welfare state, only to scale it down on the theory that the nation can no longer afford its original size. It tolerates divorce and abortion, if most of its members drew the line on gay marriage, and Sarkozy as hyper-president nevertheless legislated changes in the constitutional mechanism of the Fifth Republic that increased the powers of the National Assembly and the Constitutional Court. However, and this is an important caveat, while on the one hand the UMP steadfastly until now has refused to have anything to do with the National Front, neither entering electoral agreements with it nor collaborating in any other way, the UMP has shamelessly tried to adapt and use its themes. As minister of the interior Sarkozy threatened to use a "kärcher," popular term for the equivalent of a high-powered cleaning hose, to clean out the immigrant suburbs of their populations of delinquents, and he echoed the FN's complaint that there are "too many immigrants in France." As president Sarkozy moved against the least-popular of the immigrants, the Roma, whose camps he demolished while he had them expelled. The Roma inhabited other EU nations, of course, and their expulsion was in violation of European regulations and drew criticism from the European Union; in his campaign against Hollande Sarkozy accordingly upped his rhetoric, proposing to challenge the Schengen agreements to which France is a party and which guarantee the free movement of peoples as well as goods across EU state frontiers.

In his blatant and obvious appeal to National Front voters in 2007 Sarkozy promised, and fulfilled his promise, to establish a Ministry for Immigration and National Identity, thus in a way validating the FN claim that the one is an explicit threat to the other. The idea that a single ministry could deal with immigration and national identity seemed to many a contradiction in terms. Nor, once in power, did Sarkozy let the matter rest. From November 2009 for three months into 2010 he organized a discussion of "Frenchness" on the internet, an exercise that most of the French, however, were too cynical to take seriously. It was the source of both criticism and mirth in the press and it came to an end prematurely after three months; a projected great debate on television on national identity presided over by the president and encompassing major intellectuals was quietly buried.

Sarkozy was a very good European in policy, however. The UMP represents the interests of a globalized French capitalism, and French capitalism very much depends on the EU. As president Sarkozy made his brief

DOI: 10.1057/9781137356918.0005

six-month term of president of the European Council the high point of his term, using his position spectacularly to interject himself as negotiator of the Russian conflict with former Soviet Republic of Georgia in the fall of 2008. Sarkozy initially sought to lead a European response to the economic crisis touched off by the failure of the Lehman financial network in 2008, capitalizing on the ideas of British prime minister Gordon Brown, and he met urgently with Chancellor Merkel in an attempt to fashion the first of what became a series of rescue attempts to manage the crisis in Greece, designed to keep Greece in the EU. Sarkozy called for the pooling of European indebtedness and a rescue package for European banks, as Hollande was to do later. Pooling of the European debt is a radical notion requiring further integration than the EU currently provides for, and Hollande was to make it a campaign issue of his own, calling for the issue of "Eurobonds" jointly guaranteed by EU members. Merkel cooperated with Sarkozy in the creation of a stabilization fund for the rescue of banks and compromised governments, but she was unwilling to put any additional burden on German taxpayers by means of debt pooling despite the enormous advantage Germany gets from the unified European currency. In exchange for gradual, always insufficient installments of what were termed "bail-outs" for Greece, the Germans called for discipline on the part of the unruly Greeks, and the Spanish and the Italians and the Portuguese eventually too, imposing a new reign of "austerity" on them all.

From putative leader of the EU, or at least the Eurozone, Sarkozy fell back upon playing what he perceived to be an equal leadership role with Mrs. Merkel in the EU, but in terms of economic power France was clearly in the junior role as it called jointly for the imposition of austerity on Europe in the interest of creating "competitiveness." And if Merkel did agree to the creation of a huge stabilization fund as financial backing for a weakened euro, she exacted a "pact of stability" on the part of the other Eurozone members which Sarkozy initialed along with the rest. France promised to get its financial house in order by limiting its deficits to 3% of Gross Domestic Product, and Sarkozy began the tortuous process of cutting government expenditures in France, reducing the size of the French bureaucracy by rehiring a single *fonctionnaire* or government worker for every two who retired or were dismissed. Renegotiation of the treaty became a campaign promise for Hollande. Sarkozy, for his part, had become "Merkozy" in recognition of his apparent subjection of French policy to German requirements.

DOI: 10.1057/9781137356918.0005

The economic crisis that hit the West in 2008 following the collapse of Lehman brothers became the turning point for the Sarkozy government and the harbinger of its subsequent defeat. Perrineau sees three possible reactions to the crisis that were reflected in the campaign. These were offered first by those candidates for change without radical remedies to propose: the two major ones were Hollande and Bayrou, both of whom seemed to be offering programs designed to minimize the suffering and see to it that it was evenly distributed with a maximum sense of justice, while awaiting the return of better times. In contrast there were two candidates who clearly identified those who in their eyes were responsible for the crisis and who promised to take visible action against clearly designated enemies: these were Le Pen and Mélenchon. Sarkozy fell into neither camp: his message of flaunting wealth and a political Right that was "décomplexée" was hardly suggestive of equally shared suffering, and while he attacked budget deficits, he could not identify the enemy, the agent causing the crisis—he had no one to blame but himself. From the outset of the campaign the result seemed pre-ordained and while Sarkozy was able to narrow the gap between himself and Hollande in the end there was no way for him to overcome it.[25]

Austerity has led to contracted growth which has been flat in the Eurozone and negative in some of the Mediterranean countries. Spain and Greece have sunk to 25% rates of unemployment while the French figure slowly rose to in excess of 10%, more than enough to compound the French sense of pessimism and national decline. Sarkozy sought to compensate for his lagging popularity by a spectacular foreign policy victory. The opportunity presented itself in Libya where a popular revolt broke out against Moamar Gaddafi. Once an international paragon, Gaddafi had in fact been behaving himself in recent years, seeking integration with the West and renouncing his nuclear ambitions. At the outset of his presidency Sarkozy invited the impulsive dictator to a state visit, allowing him amid much publicity to pitch his tents on the Elysée grounds. This lent a whiff of hypocrisy to Sarkozy's policy when he appeared later as champion of the international effort to unseat the dictator and install the Libyan insurgents into power. Sarkozy relied on NATO in the campaign against Libya, and he restored tight military relations with the United States, another hallmark of his presidency. President Obama was content to stay in the background limiting the American role to logistical support as Sarkozy and the British led NATO airstrikes on behalf of the Libyan insurgents. The campaign took longer than anticipated, but Gaddafi eventually was forced from

DOI: 10.1057/9781137356918.0005

Tripoli and killed while trying to escape. Sarkozy got his victory, but it was hardly enough to save his presidency.

Sarkozy's administration was also wracked with scandal, and like his predecessor, Jacques Chirac, he faced possible indictment once he no longer enjoyed immunity from prosecution.[26] One charge was related to Gaddafi, several of whose lieutenants claimed to have transferred funds to Sarkozy during the presidential campaign of 2007 for use by the UMP. A second charge related to an alleged meeting with Liliane Bettencourt, heiress of the L'Oréal cosmetics fortune, who reportedly passed wads of cash to Sarkozy for illegal political purposes. There were further charges of personal involvement in other recurring scandals, one named for Karachi, involving bribes paid for arms contracts in Pakistan, another involving alleged favoritism on behalf of Bernard Tapie, a corrupt businessman who managed to drag both of the major political parties through the mud. Scandals appeared to have become an institutionalized aspect of French politics ever since the Panama Canal scandal in the 19th century which preceded the Dreyfus Affair and the Stavisky scandal in the 1930s that gave rise to fascist riots followed by the Popular Front.[27] The French appear to take them with a grain of salt. But as outgoing president in 2012 Sarkozy faced possible prosecution that clouded his future political career.

Notes

1 See the tables in the Appendix for a list of candidates and results.
2 Personal interview, Valérie Lafon, June 28, 2013.
3 See Laure Equy, "une de 'Libé': la droite crie à la désinformation," *Libération*, April 25, 2005. Specifically Sarkozy said Le Pen was "compatible avec la République."
4 Pascal Perrineau, *Le Symptôme Le Pen: Radiographie des électeurs du Front national* (Paris: Fayard, 1997); Nonna Mayer, *Ces Français qui votent Le Pen* (Paris: Flammarion, 2002).
5 Perrineau, *Le Symptôme Le Pen*, pp. 21–49.
6 This is not to say that Veil's Jewishness played any role in the debate, but rather that her identification with the law could well have fueled the National Front's anti-Semitism.
7 Alexandre Dézé, *Le Front National: à la conquête du pouvoir?* (Paris: Armand Colin, 2012), pp. 75–90.

DOI: 10.1057/9781137356918.0005

8   Peter Davies, *The National Front in France: Ideology, Discourse and Power* (London: Routledge, 1999).

9   Martin Schain, *The Politics of Immigration in France, Britain, and the United States* (New York: Palgrave Macmillan, 2008; second edition, 2012).

10   "Les Musulmans Français votent à gauche," *Le Figaro*, August 7, 2013.

11   Jérome Fourquet, "Des Votes Juifs," IFOP and *CEVIPOF* study, March 2012.

12   *Y-Net World News* (from Israel) put the number of French Jews voting for Sarkozy at 92.8%. May 7, 2002.

13   Mayer, *Ces Français qui votent Le Pen.*

14   Cautrès, in Pascal Perrineau, *La Décision électorale en 2012* (Paris: Armand Colin, 2013), p. 109.

15   Pietro Ignazi, "Un nouvel acteur politique," in Nonna Mayer and Pascal Perrineau, *Le Front National à Découvert* (Paris: Presses de la Fondation Nationale des Sciences Politiques, 1989), pp. 37–63.

16   Mayer, *Ces Français qui votent Le Pen*, pp. 231–249.

17   Although nationalist and populist, the quote, from *L'Aiglon*, by Edmond Rostand also constituted a subtle appeal to the more educated to join the FN.

18   Dézé, *Le Front National*, pp. 129–154.

19   Jean-Luc Mano, *Les Phrases chocs de la campagne présidentielle* (Paris: Jean-Claude Gawsewitch, 2012), p. 16.

20   The results are most easily accessed on *Wikipedia*, French Presidential Elections, 2012.

21   *Le Monde*, April 23, 2012.

22   Jean-François Kahn, *La Catastrophe du 6 Mai 2012* (Paris: Plon, 2012).

23   On the Sarkozy presidency good summaries may be found in Gino Reymond, ed., *The Sarkozy Presidency: Breaking the Mold* (New York: Palgrave-Macmillan, 2013).

24   These strands may be regarded as inheritors of the three traditional strands of the French Right identified in his classic work by René Rémond. The best study of the UMP is by Florence Haegel, *Les Droites en fusion; Transformations de l'UMP* (Paris: Presses de la Fondation Nationale des Sciences Politiques, 2012).

25   Perrineau, *La Décision électorale*, pp. 185–187.

26   Philip Gourevitch, "Can Nicolas Sarkozy—and France—Survive the European Crisis?" *The New Yorker*, September 12, 2011.

27   See Paul Jankowski, *Shades of Indignation: Political Scandals in France Past and Present* (New York: Berghahn Books, 2008).

DOI: 10.1057/9781137356918.0005

3
The Campaign and the Elections

Abstract: *The campaign was desultory. Hollande managed to kick off his campaign with what seemed a coherent set of proposals for the economic revival of the country. Sarkozy attacked his opponent as a non-entity and turned his attention to the nationalistic themes of anti-immigration, promising to require the labeling of halal meat as his police expelled the Roma. The real underlying problem of troubled minority suburban communities suffering the ravages of unemployment remained unaddressed. Similarly ignored was foreign policy in particular, the euro crisis, which injected itself into the French campaign through the more and more frequent calls for austerity. It was not clear how Hollande would carry out his campaign promises while balancing the budget.*

Wall, Irwin. *France Votes: The Election of François Hollande.* New York: Palgrave Macmillan, 2014. DOI: 10.1057/9781137356918.0006.

The election campaign itself was desultory. Hollande opened his campaign formally in January 2012, unveiling 60 propositions for the rejuvenation of France. The scene was an airplane hangar at Le Bourget airport, the speech had been a long time in preparation, and Hollande by most accounts rose to the occasion. His proposals engaged the entire gamut of French society running from investment banks to job training, housing, medicine, employment, education, security, energy, and the like. The package of measures was calculated to estimated cost, and allegedly could be funded by prospective minimal changes in the tax code.[1] Hollande promised not to increase the deficit; on the contrary he would bring the budget into balance over his five-year term. Most notably the candidate promised to attack the employment problem by employing 150,000 young people, apprenticing them to those approaching retirement in what he called a "contract of generations," and adding 60,000 posts to the system of secondary and higher education. He promised to reduce France's dependence on nuclear energy for its electricity from 75 to 50%, and to expand investment in renewable energy such as solar and wind power. He addressed reform of institutions, pledging to abolish the system of multiple offices held by a single person (it has always been common in France for deputies in the National Assembly to also be mayors of the leading cities in their regions at the same time, for example). He promised to modify the electoral system so as to include a dose of proportional representation into legislative elections, allowing all parties with a minimum vote to enjoy at least some representation in the National Assembly. He proposed to increase the powers of the National Assembly and promised to respect the role of the prime minister as the head of the government and of the majority in the parliament. Sarkozy was accused of have turned the prime minister into an assistant of the president. A less popular measure Hollande listed was his intention to give the vote in municipal elections to legal residents of France who were not citizens. All these reforms were again meant to address perceived political crisis. He would expand social freedoms, allowing gays to marry and to adopt children.

Hollande's speech was well-delivered, his plans sounded measured and achievable, and by all accounts, perhaps for the first time, he impressed his listeners with the seriousness of his candidacy. His proposals, however, added up for the most part to cosmetic changes insufficient to deal with the scale of the crisis, unless he succeeded in restoring growth-oriented policies in the Eurozone, bringing an end to austerity. He terminated his

DOI: 10.1057/9781137356918.0006

speech with a resounding note, yet a new borrowing from the United States: he offered his countrymen the chance to realize "le rêve français," the French dream, although he did not explain how it might resemble or differ from its American counterpart.[2] In fact the French appeared rather confused about what it might mean: for the Right it ought to have its American connotation, a society in which there is equal opportunity for each individual to get ahead; but for the Left in France it meant the preservation of what was hard-earned and already achieved, a welfare state infused with the ideals of social justice and compassion.[3] Hollande started the campaign with an overwhelming lead in the polls, about 10%, which did not appear to narrow until the very final weeks of the campaign. From very early on it did not seem that he could be beaten.

Nevertheless, Sarkozy criticized his opponent as a non-entity, depicting Hollande as someone severely lacking the capacity for statesmanship. He emphasized his nationalist themes of defining French identity and controlling France's borders in a blatant appeal for the anti-immigrant vote. Sarkozy promised to reduce immigration by half in the next five years. He would prevent immigrants from entering France simply to take advantage of its extensive social benefits. In an impromptu reply to a charge by Marine Le Pen that all meat sold in Paris was being slaughtered according to "halal" requirements (a Muslim ritual), Sarkozy insisted on the labeling of halal meat; the French have the right to know what they are eating, he said. To compound the issue, Prime Minister Fillon went on to question the appropriateness of Jewish and Muslim methods of slaughtering meat altogether, prompting a protest by France's Grand Rabbi.[1] These blatantly prejudiced pronouncements brought a sarcastic reply from Mélenchon, who observed that "you don't catch Islam by eating it." Sarkozy of course had a personal history with the Muslim ghettos in the suburbs, but now he also had a record of five years of doing little about them. His themes rang hollow after five years of his presidency, during which the suburbs were unchanged while his economic policies of quasi-austerity and his foreign policy of alignment with Angela Merkel in Europe resulted in widespread unpopularity.

The suburbs around Paris drew an enormous amount of attention during the riots and car burnings that took place there, peaking in 2005 and continuing sporadically since, yet they were barely otherwise mentioned during the campaign. On one level they are a non-issue because nobody has a plan for dealing with them. On the other hand it is easy to deduce that they do not deserve the attention they get. Cergy,

DOI: 10.1057/9781137356918.0006

northwest of Paris, for example, reveals almost tastefully constructed publicly financed apartment buildings in rather good condition at modest rents, in a community that admittedly is not the usual suburb; the town also houses both a university and a prefecture. Neither of these, however, have much to do with the immigrant community, which is geographically quite separate from them in the subsidized public housing, and thus typical of suburbs elsewhere.[5]

On a Wednesday one may see in Cergy an active and colorful market, with ordinary French people mixing with a wide variety of immigrants in native dress, mostly from Africa and the Middle East. The produce is attractive and plentiful with purchases being wrapped and money changing hands at a furious rate. An American cannot help but marvel at the relative absence in this French ghetto of anything approaching the visual poverty one can often see in the United States, and it bears remembering that all the immigrant populations in France enjoy free medical care as do the rest of the French. Of course the effects of the ravages of unemployment are not visible in the daily activities of the population, nor are the anger and frustration that the absence of jobs creates. Cars are occasionally torched on weekends, reflecting anger at ghettoization and the lack of adequate affordable transportation to paying jobs, and France has not done much to end discrimination. A group of all-white young policemen, heavily armed, eying their charges warily at the fringes of the market, hardly appears encouraging in terms of race relations. The police insist, however, that their program of "proximité" keeps them in close touch with influential persons in the immigrant community. A resident sums up the effect of five years of Sarkozy's presidency, however, in the ubiquitous visibility of security cameras.

The campaign was interrupted by the terrorist assault on three French soldiers of North African ethnicity and then the shooting of several Jewish children at a religious school in Toulouse on March 19, 2012. The initial reaction was the suspicion that the extreme Right was responsible, but it was Bayrou, not Hollande, who prematurely indicted Sarkozy as accountable for the incidents by fomenting a climate of hate in the country with his campaign tactics.[6] Hollande remained silent, and was rewarded for having done so when the killer turned out to be Mohamed Merah, a would-be Algerian jihadist. Sarkozy enjoyed the limelight uncontested while taking charge of Merah's apprehension; but the incident had no discernible impact on the polls.

DOI: 10.1057/9781137356918.0006

Sarkozy had never recovered from the precipitous fall in popularity he suffered early in his presidency when he first earned the moniker of "president bling-bling." Like presidents before him, he was unable to do anything about the high rate of unemployment. France continued to suffer the effect of "la crise," which ravaged all of Europe except Germany since 2008, and as a consequence of which governments have regularly been thrown out of office in Europe's democracies, 16 of them by *Le Monde*'s count in the three years preceding the elections in France.[7] Nor did it matter to electorates whether the offending governments were of the Right or the Left. It would have been exceptional had Sarkozy won in these conditions.

Sarkozy's desperation showed up in his radical turn to the Right during his campaign. Sarkozy returned to the issue of national identity again and again, clearly defining Muslims and immigrants as the "other."[8] The government stepped up its hard line against illegal immigration and carried out orchestrated expulsions of immigrants, especially the Roma. The president went so far as to question France's future adherence to the Schengen agreement which stipulates the free movement of persons with the adhering countries of the EU. But it was all to no avail. Polls anticipating the second ballot continued after the first ballot to predict a victory for Holland of 54% to 46%, well outside the so-called margins of error.

Hollande campaigned on economic and social issues, promising to undo Sarkozy's lowering of the retirement age from 62 to 60 and to increase taxes on the rich while achieving a greater measure of economic and social equality. He borrowed a page from the Left of a bygone era when he declared that his adversary was the world of finance capitalism. On the other hand he reminded the electorate that a previous government of the Left, that of Jospin, had been friendly to privatizations and a market economy. Perhaps the most notorious of Hollande's proposals was that of a tax of 75% to be levied on all incomes above one million euros. Hollande recognized that this would in fact bring little additional revenue to the treasury, but he justified it on the grounds of shared sacrifice, calling upon the rich to show their patriotism by agreeing to this additional contribution. Hollande also widely advertised the idea that he would be a "normal" president, perhaps a welcome contrast to his opponent's mercurial style and yet a way of emphasizing his own lack of dynamism and charisma as a virtue. What he meant by "normal" was perhaps deliberately left ambivalent, however: did he mean the term to

DOI: 10.1057/9781137356918.0006

denote that he would exercise the presidency rather as other presidents had done in opposition to the erratic style of Sarkozy, or was he referring to his own personality as "normal" as opposed to the actual president, who was not normal in the sense of mentally unstable? On one occasion, asked to explain what "normal" meant, Hollande explained that he simply meant an approachable president; he was not one of the elite, rather one of the people.[9]

Foreign policy was all but absent from the campaign as an issue. Neither candidate offered any new or different policy to deal with the Syrian civil war, Iran's nuclear ambitions, or French policy in the NATO alliance. They did not disagree on any of these questions, and Hollande endorsed Sarkozy's single foreign policy adventure, the lead role France played in the ousting of the Libyan dictator Gaddafi. Hollande promised the definitive end to "Françafrique," the peculiar relationship that France appears to have maintained with its former colonies. France maintains several thousand troops in Africa and they occasionally intervene in the politics of the nations of the former French Union. Sarkozy protested, however, arguing that Françafrique no longer existed in any case. But Hollande was to conduct his own intervention in Mali soon after he came to power, and that was followed by an intervention in the Central African Republic. With or without Françafrique, Hollande followed the tradition of French activism and intervention in its former African colonies.

Pascal Perrineau, a leading French political commentator and analyst, observes somewhat sarcastically that Hollande may have won because of who he was not rather than who he was. He was the anti–Dominique Strauss-Kahn, lacking the latter's taste for luxury, economic expertise, and sexual deviance; he was the anti–Martine Aubry, whom he bested in the primary, jovially lacking her seemingly permanent scowl, reputation as a party enforcer of discipline, and avatar of sectarianism. But most of all Hollande was the anti–Nicolas Sarkozy.[10] He would restore the balanced sense of deliberation and consultation necessary to the presidency in contrast to his opponent, who rushed about making arbitrary decisions without follow-up. And if he did not replicate the quasi-monarchical style of his predecessors as president, he did share with them deep roots in the national soil. Sarkozy was the strange, exotic, and Parisian ethnic mix of Hungarian, French, Greek, and Jewish backgrounds, while Hollande was issue of "la France profonde." Hollande made much of his roots in the Corrèze, where he became president of the local council and developed close ties with

DOI: 10.1057/9781137356918.0006

another famous resident, Sarkozy's predecessor Jacques Chirac. Chirac said at one point that he intended to vote for Hollande, a statement that the UMP tried to explain away, saying that it either reflected his confusion or was meant in jest. Given Chirac's personal dislike of Sarkozy, however, the remark was probably meant to be taken at face value.[11]

If anything the result of the election appeared over-determined, which somewhat diminishes the achievement of political science "modelers" who some four months earlier "modeled" the election and predicted its result with accuracy.[12] It was Hollande's election to win; Sarkozy had already done everything he could to lose it. Missing from the campaign were the proverbial "issues"; foreign policy was hardly discussed outside of Europe, and the nature of Europe's deep and profound economic doldrums and the crisis of the Euro that seemed to portend dire consequences for all, not only Greece, was more the subject of polemic than serious proposals for problem-solving. Hollande promised to renegotiate the recently initialed European pact for economic stability so as to include a component stressing a joint commitment to economic growth. He also called for EU-backed "Eurobonds," which could have collectively financed the debt, but as mentioned, the German government vehemently rejected the proposal. Endorsement of an activist campaign to save the euro, undertaken by the European bank under the leadership of Mario Draghi, rounded out his prescriptions.

On its cover of March 31, 2012, *The Economist* (Figure 3.1) caused a minor sensation by depicting the campaign as reflecting the frivolous mood of Manet's famous painting, the "Déjeuner sur l'herbe," in which two impeccably dressed bourgeois gentlemen enjoy a picnic lunch on a lawn in the presence of an alluring and naked lady whose presence they seem to be either unaware of or to ignore while another demurely dressed bather soaks her feet in the background. *The Economist's* version of the painting was a composite photograph that superimposed the faces of Sarkozy and Hollande on the bodies of the male picnickers.[13] France was in denial, charged the magazine; the economic proposals of the candidates were each more risky and stupid than those of the other, and both ignored the real problem symbolized by the naked lady in the painting, there but ignored. The photo was reproduced and commented upon in *Le Monde* and the French press generally, but clever as it may have been it is doubtful that the *Economist* offered better remedies. It said that Hollande's putative war on finance capital and his 75% tax on incomes over one million euros threatened an exodus from France of the

DOI: 10.1057/9781137356918.0006

most competent and productive of its citizens, while Sarkozy was incapable of envisaging the structural reforms or radical cuts in government expenditure that the crisis demanded. France was ignoring the putative cause of its decline, its lack of competitiveness. In other words, the cure for a failed policy of austerity for the *Economist* was an even stronger dose of austerity.

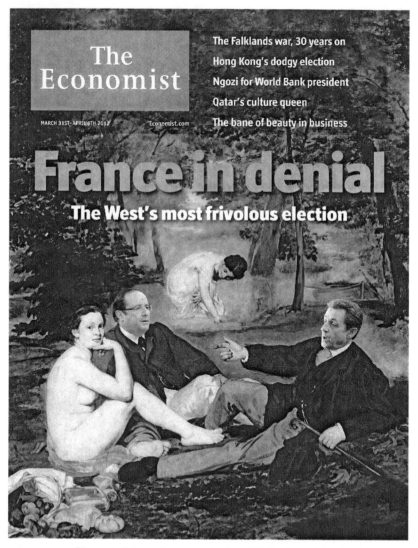

FIGURE 3.1   *"France's future; A country in denial," The Economist, March 31, 2012*

DOI: 10.1057/9781137356918.0006

The Economist attacked from the right, Paul Krugman from the left. Krugman railed against austerity in the *New York Times*, targeting as its worst example David Cameron in Britain, but noting that its ravages were being forced on the European continent by Angela Merkel with the complicity of Sarkozy. Austerity harkened back to the Great Depression, said Krugman. It hid a reactionary agenda behind a bad metaphor.[14] The metaphor was to compare the state's budget with that of an individual householder obliged to balance income against expenses. The role of the state was in fact the opposite: to increase expenses during economic downturns, using only boom times to impose austerity. Behind their bad metaphor, warned Krugman, were forces seeking the withering of the state role in the economy, the fraying if not the destruction of the welfare state by using the budget deficit and the supposed need to balance it in an effort to dismantle social programs. This was the obvious program of American Republicans, noted Krugman.

But the candidates did not so much ignore the crisis of the euro as they attempted a precarious balancing act, given the increasing unpopularity of the European Union in France. The disillusionment showed in several obvious ways. At one point Sarkozy admitted that Europe had been meant to protect its members from globalization but had instead further exposed them to its ravages. France, as a corporate economy and one of the world's largest industrial powers, is heavily involved in and dependent on globalization. Its economy thrives on exports and its foreign investment is massive, including widespread holdings in the United States almost equivalent to the investments held by Americans in France. Once hostile to foreign investment in France, the country today actively tries to encourage it. Yet globalization is more unpopular in France than in any other nation and is blamed for a wide variety of ills. It has often been observed that the country that attacked McDonald's and vandalized its locales was the country in which McDonald's made the most profits.

Globalization injected itself into the campaign through the issue of jobs that were exported as corporations fled France to find lower wages for manufacturing abroad. Marine Le Pen remarked sarcastically that globalization was a system in which slave labor abroad manufactured items at prices low enough for the resulting unemployed workers in France to purchase them. The candidates promised to reverse the trend: Hollande announced that he would be the president of industrial recovery and renewed productivity. He promised to restore the

DOI: 10.1057/9781137356918.0006

competitiveness of French industry. He would introduce a new fiscal regime imbued with a greater sense of social justice. And his would be a policy of employment.[15]

Sarkozy, on the other hand, had focused his presidency on budget balancing, reducing spending while at the same time seeking to reduce taxes, the policy widely known as austerity, or as the French called it, *rigueur*. Austerity and a politics of recovered competitiveness were widely advertised as having been the remedy for German economic recovery and were imposed on the Eurozone as the antidote to the euro crisis afflicting the southern economies of Greece, Italy, Spain, Portugal, and Cyprus. It was vigorously denounced in the *New York Times* by Paul Krugman as being a crude throwback to the depression era politics of Herbert Hoover, Stanley Baldwin, and Pierre Laval, the consequence of which was increased unemployment. The Keynesian era of spending one's way to recovery had lost ground in Europe and America since the era of Reagan and Thatcher in the 1980s, however.

The Franco-German tandem under the Sarkozy presidency, often referred to as "Merkozy," had prescribed and enforced the policy upon all of the Eurozone, and the crisis of the euro in turn injected itself into the French campaign. Under Sarkozy's urging Merkel avoided meeting with Hollande even during his trips to Germany when he met with Social-Democratic leaders there. She made clear her support for Sarkozy, and Sarkozy declared he was proud to have it. *Le Monde* in fact speculated about a virtual cabal against Hollande's candidature in Europe by the leaders of England, Germany, Italy, and Spain, all under conservative political leadership.

Hollande for his part declined to criticize austerity even as he sought to modify its implementation in France. Like all French politicians he excoriated the debt and promised to bring the French state budget into balance by the end of his term as president. Hollande's use of the code words in "rebuilding" French industry and restoring the "competitive-ness" of French labor seemed only promises of further austerity, however; how was industry to be prevented from departing for foreign climes in pursuit of lower production costs in the context of the EU, free trade, and globalization? What could competitiveness mean other than stagnant or falling wages and tax hikes to cover the cost of reducing the social costs of hiring for French enterprises? As far as the budget was concerned, "the debt is the enemy of the left," declared Hollande's future economics minister Pierre Moscovici. It would be difficult to find a more foolish

DOI: 10.1057/9781137356918.0006

declaration during the campaign, yet it seemed to reflect popular belief among the French electorate, which consistently put the nation's indebtedness on a par with the economic crisis and resulting unemployment as the most serious of the nation's problems. Before dealing with the remainder of the campaign and the elections themselves we must detour here to examine the problems of France in relation to the Eurozone.

Notes

1   *Le Monde*, January 16, 2012.

2   Claude Estier, *Journal d'une victoire* (Paris: Cherche-Midi, 2012), pp. 109–112.

3   Françoise Fressoz, « L'indéfinissable rêve français », *Le Monde*, April 12, 2012, blog.

4   "Sarkozy: le halal. 'premier sujet des préoccupations des Français,'" *Le Nouvel Observateur*, March 5, 2012.

5   Beth Epstein, *Collective Terms: Race, Culture & Community in a State-Planned City in France* (London and New York: Berghahn Books, 2011). Beth Epstein was kind enough to guide me through the immigrant-inhabited areas and market of Cergy on June 20, 2012.

6   "Fusillade de Toulouse: François Bayrou accuse les responsables politiques... et égratigne Sarkozy," *Le Point*, March 20, 2012.

7   *Le Monde*, April 20, 2012.

8   The debate took place on the internet and lasted from November 2, 2009, until February 2, 2010.

9   Laurent Binet, *Rien ne se passe comme prévu* (Paris: Grasset, 2012). Binet, a novelist, was invited by Hollande to write an "insider" account of the campaign.

10 Pascal Perrineau, personal interview, June 26, 2012. See his *Politics in France and Europe* (New York: Palgrave Macmillan, 2009) and *Le Choix de Marianne: Pourquoi et pour qui votons nous?* (Paris: Fayard, 2012).

11 Serge Raffy, *François Hollande: itinéraire secret* (Paris: Fayard, 2012).

12 See the Research Symposium: Forecasting the French Elections, *French Politics* 10, 1 (April 2012), online at http://www.palgrave-journals.com/fp/journal/v10/n1/index.html.

13 "'La Partie Carrée'—'The Economist' raille une France 'dans le déni,'" *Le Monde*, March 30, 2012.

14 Paul Krugman, "The Austerity Agenda," *The New York Times*, May 31, 2012.

15 Alain Bergounioux, "Le changement pour maintenant... et pour demain," *La Revue Socialiste*, 45–46 (2011), 4–6.

DOI: 10.1057/9781137356918.0006

4
France and the Euro Crisis

Abstract: *The euro crisis, little discussed, profoundly affected the elections in France and the policy options available to candidates. Hollande appeared conscious of this and constrained his campaign promises accordingly. The nations in the Eurozone sacrificed a major component of sovereignty when they abandoned their ability to control their currencies to a European Central Bank itself run under conditions of stringent anti-inflationary policies. The Eurozone, created at a time of anti-inflationary consensus in Europe in the 1990s, imposes a kind of obligatory austerity on its members by requiring budgets balanced to within 3% of GDP and national debt limits under 60% of GDP. Socialist economists offered copious recommendations in reaction to the depression that began in 2008 and that manifested itself in the Eurozone in the sovereign debt crisis. They backed Hollande and counseled him to rethink the role of the state, reorder labor relations, and introduce German and Scandinavian-type "flexicurity" in employment. Thomas Piketty's work revealed the deleterious effects of growing inequality and advocated aggressive policies of taxation and redistribution to mitigate its effects. But few questioned the Eurozone or its policies of austerity, least of all Hollande.*

Wall, Irwin. *France Votes: The Election of François Hollande.* New York: Palgrave Macmillan, 2014.
DOI: 10.1057/9781137356918.0007.

Debt is the enemy of neither the Left nor the Right, and one can no more make war against deficits than one can conduct a war against terror. Terror is itself an arm of warfare. Debt is an arm of economic policy, a valued and necessary source of government revenue as it is a needed source of investment in the private sector. Traditionally the national debt is a safer vehicle for public saving than anything available in the public sector and that tends to be reflected in lower interest rates on government bonds. In fact, paradoxically, French interest rates during the campaign on the debt were among the lowest in the nation's recorded history, in the 2.5% range on the standard ten-year note. This reflected investor confidence in the financial solvency of France, and it enabled the government to carry a much larger debt than it had earlier at the same or even lower cost. In fact with the interest rate in the country roughly at the inflation rate, the debt was almost cost-free. Under these conditions, Keynesian economists argued, the state should be enlarging the debt and injecting the increased revenue into the economy in the form of public investment to spur economic growth. The constraints against doing so, however, lay in the policies of the Eurozone.

The strictures imposed by the founders of the single currency reflected the extreme anti-inflationary doctrines and practices of the Federal Republic of Germany at the time of the joint currency's adoption in the early 1990s. Germany has been allergic to inflation since the immediate postwar period when a consensus developed blaming the great inflation of the post–First World War period for the rise of Hitler. In fact the inflation was long since over and had given way to the Great Depression when the Nazi movement became a mass movement. Unemployment and deflation were the conditions under which Hitler came to power, not inflation. This argument was pointedly and repeatedly made by higher-ups in the PS, who chafed at the European Bank's primary goal being the prevention of inflation rather than encouraging growth. They argued that the postwar inflation rather brought about the conditions for the prosperity that took hold during the Weimar era. Be that as it may, German banking practices have since put a premium on currency stability, associating inflation with the slapdash economic policies of the Latin countries of Europe and Greece, and equating it with disaster for Germany. France too had overused inflation, and its leaders joined in the anti-inflationary consensus that accompanied the birth of the euro in the 1990s.[1]

Germany's rigidity caused turmoil and failure during early efforts to create a European monetary system in the 1980s. The strength of the mark set the standard to which everyone else had to adjust. Even successive revaluations of the mark upward did not change the reality of Germany's positive trade balances. The German economy benefits from a virtual monopoly on crucial types of manufacturing, a superbly educated labor force, and an all but strike-free economy. Labor was once and for all broken in Germany by the Nazi experience and then co-opted by the ingenious postwar system of Mitbestimmung or co-management during the postwar period. The powerful German labor unions since the postwar period have enjoyed representation of their workers on the boards and management councils of their enterprises. The pressure for the establishment of the euro, however, paradoxically came from Germany's partners, in particular the French, who needed a means to bind Germany further to Europe in the aftermath of the fall of communism and the resulting German reunification, and who hoped that a common currency would lessen the ability of Germany to dictate economic policy in Europe and further integration. Their hopes in the latter respect have been dashed, and the euro, rather than bind Europe together, has seemed to be driving it apart.

The euro was an extraordinary forfeit of sovereignty on the part of the nations that subscribed to it. Nations have three ways of creating revenue: taxes, borrowing, and purchases of government debt by their national banks, or in a word, inflation. In the United States, the Federal Reserve can purchase newly issued government debt, but the European Central Bank (ECB) is statutorily unable to do so. The EU does not issue any debt and the ECB may not buy bonds issued by the member countries. Instead it has resorted to limited lending of funds to banks at 1%, allowing the banks to purchase debt from the member countries at 5% interest. When the Federal Reserve or the ECB purchases government debt, this results in the creation of new money or inflation, although in the current crisis in the United States a new name has been invented for it, "quantitative easing." The creation of the euro meant the sacrifice by each nation of its individual ability to resort to inflation, including currency devaluation for competitive advantage, and these tools in the past were common ways of accumulation and growth in France, Spain, and Italy in different periods. The Eurozone is unable to issue debt itself, and the ECB is unable to purchase the debt of its members, but it has found the means of forcing policies of austerity on them. Yet it lacks the power and the means to adopt a contrary policy of economic stimulus even if it wished to do so. With the creation of the euro the nations

DOI: 10.1057/9781137356918.0007

adopting it were thus committing themselves permanently to currency stability. Germany insisted, moreover, on a set of domestic policies designed to enforce stability: member countries must limit their budget deficits to 3% of Gross Domestic Product (GDP) and their national debt to 60% of GDP. These arbitrary limits, which up to now the member nations have frequently violated, are given more teeth in the new Pact of Stability that the Eurozone nations have adopted in reaction to the current euro crisis.

Inflation has been described as an "unscientific means of taxation"; it accomplished the transfer of wealth from one segment of society to another, which is the purpose of taxation, but it forced adjustments for everyone and struggles among different groups to emerge from it advantageously. It can be a vehicle for the peaceful conduct of class conflict and its resolution. It can also lead to chaos when practiced to excess, as often was the case in Argentina or elsewhere in South America, and of course the illustrative case of postwar Germany.[2] The postwar German inflation of 1919–1923 was arguably the worst in history. Some might argue that France was a culprit too in the overuse of inflation; when de Gaulle brought the postwar era of French inflation to an end in 1958 he created a new franc by simply lopping off two zeros from the value of the old. One hundred old francs became one new franc, and one old franc became a centime. But the French economy had achieved remarkable recovery and growth under the Fourth Republic by resorting to inflation.

The euro creates a kind of conservative straitjacket into which the participating economies are inserted. Bereft of the vehicle of currency adjustment they must tax or borrow in order to spend—they have surrendered the power to print money. And it often seems since the 1980s that they have lost the political power to tax as well. As Thomas Piketty shows in *Capital in the Twenty-First Century*, while the European nations are very rich, their governments are very poor, indebted beyond their assets which some of them are being forced to sell to satisfy lenders. Given the stringencies of existing capital markets, moreover, their capacity to borrow depends in turn on interest rates and the judgments of rating agencies about their ability to repay. The rating agencies use the criteria of deficits and the volume of national debt to make their judgments. This means in turn a permanent politics of austerity: governments remain under continuous pressure to keep budgets more or less in balance and face limitations on their ability to build infrastructure, further investment, or carry out social reform. The euro was instituted, moreover, during the 1990s, a particularly propitious time for the development of economic conservatism built upon a neo-liberal capitalist consensus.[3]

There are those who argue that neo-liberalism, or more specifically the Hayekian doctrines of limitations on state power over the economy, always underlay the philosophic assumptions that created the Common Market back during the period of the Treaty of Rome in 1957. Others stress the doctrine of "ordo-liberalism" which more specifically refers to the German social market economy of the postwar that calls for the state to play a role in regulating competition, providing for a fair market economy, and leaves room for the "social" measures associated with state intervention on behalf of the disadvantaged.[4] The Common Market and the European project that resulted in the present structure of the EU have in the past been pushed forward by Christian Democrats and Socialists as well as ordo- or neo-liberals, and European unity has also been fueled by the internal politics of the member states who felt able to strengthen themselves individually by pooling several of their functions together.[5] Geo-politics were as or more important than economics in the creation of the EU, which has contributed to a half-century of peace and the spread of political democracy by example since the end of the Second World War. Nevertheless, Bernard Moss warns us against conferring upon the EU a kind of "sanctity" which puts it above criticism. For Moss the euro has become a mechanism for the enforcement of neo-liberal nostrums on the members of the Eurozone, forcing them to cut back on their welfare states at the cost of economic growth in an ideologically driven assault on government intervention in the economy.[6] More specifically it severely limited the options open to François Hollande as he challenged the economic policies of Nicolas Sarkozy in the French elections of 2012.

In fact since the Single European Act of 1986 and the Maastricht Treaty the regulation of capitalism on the continent has come to appear to be the EU's central function. Capital and money cross frontiers freely and need to be regulated by a central authority. But the EU has no corresponding social presence in Europe other than a charter of principles to which not all its members subscribe. The regulation of labor and the income transfers of the welfare state take place through the national states, which play a much larger role in the national economies of their countries than the EU. The individual governments in their control of their national economies range from 35% to 55% (France being the largest); the EU budget is tiny by comparison and accounts for only about 1.5% of the GDP of the

DOI: 10.1057/9781137356918.0007

entire European Union. The EU functions very modestly as an agent of transfer; it does invest from its tax base in individually targeted regions of the Union for purposes of fostering their development, but it is not a central redistributive authority as are the national governments in the EU member countries. Aside from its regulation of capitalism, the EU has taken on a very great regulatory role in terms of the environment and other issues common to the member states, although it must rely on the individual states for compliance. And the jurisprudence of its international court, which pushes strongly for human rights, tends to be respected and implemented by the national courts of the member states as well. But it remains the case that capitalism is European in the old world while the welfare of its workers is the concern of the individual national states. A "social" Europe, which is the stated goal of a candidate like Mélenchon, and to which Hollande also gives lip service, is very far from becoming a reality. Indeed, Mélenchon, in his campaign and after, called for "another Europe, founded on a popular base, social and solidary (communal)" as opposed to the current Europe that is neo-liberal and individualistic.[7] The absence of a "popular base" means the EU is a top down structure with little direct access to the people, who participate in politics nationally; power in the EU lies in the Commission and the Council and the popularly elected European parliament has very little influence. Hence the common lament about the EU's alleged "democratic deficit."

Hollande was aware of the economic constraints he would face during his campaign for the presidency; to believe Bernard Bergounioux he did not think that once in power he would be able to overcome them entirely. Nor did he think the constraints of austerity could or should be entirely dispensed with. He rather shared the consensus that has emerged around their necessity. He wanted to renegotiate the stability pact, adding to it a clause on the necessity for growth, and allocating some funds from the European stability fund to be invested in public works designed to stimulate growth. But the scale of his proposal, on the order of 130 billion euros, to be shared among 17 countries, was very modest. The American stimulus passed by the Obama administration amounted to 830 billion dollars, the American economy being about equivalent of that of the entire European Union. But not only was Hollande's stimulus proposal modest, he did not advocate abandoning the stability treaty and once in power he forced his party to ratify it. On the one hand Hollande knew that if France were to continue on Sarkozy's trajectory of reducing the deficit growth would be inhibited instead of encouraged in the short run.

DOI: 10.1057/9781137356918.0007

But Hollande also was aware that the Left is in the minority in France and that to win he needed votes from the Center and the Right. And once elected, of course, he needed to be president of all the French. For Bergounioux the Socialists faced governing with a kind of fatal sense of necessity; they would have no choice but to govern in hard times at cost to themselves, hoping by their compassion and concern for social justice to achieve a sense of "apaisement," literally calming, or appeasement among the population while the nation struggled through its necessary period of social hardship and austerity.[8]

The euro crisis had already dragged on for several years prior to the election and it continued afterward. It was dealt with on a kind of ad hoc basis by the powers that be in the Eurozone. Whenever it came to a boiling point there was a crisis meeting for another "fix," or bailout of the afflicted economy: Greece, Ireland, Cyprus, Spain, and Portugal were the immediate problems that flared up but all had their eyes on Italy, whose economy was large enough to threaten the entire Union and which could not be allowed to fail. In essence the euro crisis was the European version of the sub-prime economic crunch that hit the United States in 2008, but it was only partially about reckless home-building and bad mortgage loans on the continent, where the crisis rather took the form of a sovereign debt debacle. Excessive loans were made to the aforementioned nations by banks in Italy, France, Germany, and the countries of Northern Europe that fueled speculative booms in housing and the like in Greece and Ireland and Spain. When the crisis hit after 2008 it appeared that the loans most likely could not be repaid.

Loan defaults were hardly unknown in international affairs in the past, and the banks should have been quite familiar with them: there was a massive sovereign debt crisis in the 1980s, for example, and Latin American nations then defaulted, causing losses in major international banks in the United States. Some of the East European Communist economies defaulted as well, having borrowed excessively prior to the economic and political collapse of 1989. In the first decade of the 21st century the appearance of the euro, however, gave the impression that loans to the nations that had adopted it were iron clad, and in fact the interest rates of the bonds of the various Eurozone countries converged, reflecting the fact that loans made in euros seemed certain to be repaid regardless of which country received them.[9] The floodgates were opened for speculative booms that took place in Greece, Ireland, Cyprus, and Spain, which were eagerly financed by banks in France and Germany.

DOI: 10.1057/9781137356918.0007

As the booms collapsed and the debts came due, banks were threatened with failure and governments rushed to their support. Then, as interest rates on government debt rose as a consequence, default loomed. The euro itself as a currency appeared to be threatened with failure.

There existed no central fiscal authority to manage the euro, so the crisis was dealt with by an ad hoc arrangement, a so-called troika consisting of the European Central Bank, the European Commission, and the International Monetary Fund. Its aim was to keep the Eurozone intact, prevent default, protect the banks, and save the euro as a currency. Plans have been developed to establish further centralized authority within the EU to supervise the banks, oversee the economies of the Eurozone members, and administer emergency funds that have been established, in particular the European Financial Stability Facility, which is managed by a newly created European Stability Mechanism. Through a series of emergency meetings precipitated by the threat of Greek defaults, bailout funds have been established to save the Greek government, but these have been made dependent on efficient tax collection by Greek authorities amid generalized tax increases.[10] Thus the cost of Greek government profligacy, a faulty tax-collection system, and reckless lending to Greece by foreign banks were passed on to the Greek people who were made to experience a deep drop in their living standard and suffer depression and unemployment amounting to 25% and more. A similar situation has been pushed upon the Spanish population, imposed by the Spanish government in an effort to stave off EU intervention and save Spanish banks, but with similar results for the Spanish people. Amid financial collapse and austerity in Spain the population is being made to pay for the profligacy of the government and the banks amid depression and unemployment totals of 25% and higher. Meanwhile throughout the Eurozone growth rates have been flat and unemployment high, with the exception of Germany and a few Nordic countries.

Germany met the threat of depression head on early in the decade by downgrading its living standards and making itself competitive in a world economy, and it has not hesitated to propound if not force the same policies on the other Eurozone nations as a remedy for their ills. Balance the budget, tighten one's belt, consume less, and confidence will return bringing renewed investment, economic activity, and a return to prosperity. But how can prosperity be restored if everyone practices austerity, depressing demand, at the same time? Nor has everyone else the kind of specialized niche economy that Germany has that apparently allows it to remain competitive despite its higher wages and production costs compared to the rest of the world.

Curiously a lone voice in the Socialist party appears to have articulated this concern, that of Arnaud de Montebourg, who ran against Hollande in the Socialist primary and won sufficient support such that Hollande felt obligated to make him minister of industrial reconstruction after the election victory. Montebourg alone dared to question the central premises of globalization. He frankly called for less, not more, world trade, and a policy that brought consumption closer to production, in many cases keeping production within the national frontiers even at higher cost to the consumer.[11] Over the long term, Montebourg said, fuel costs are likely to rise, making long distance shipping expensive, even as it added immeasurably to international pollution. The existing policy of exporting production to countries of low-cost labor is not environmentally sustainable, especially in the producing countries themselves. Montebourg further castigated China for its selfish and oppressive labor policies; he called China an autocracy that disallowed the free organization of labor, a nation of "quasi-slavery and dictatorship" that also recklessly ignored environmental constraints, hoarded its surplus trade balances, amassing holdings of trillions of dollars while refusing to allow a decent level of consumption to its own citizens. Montebourg thus, in his own way, echoed Le Pen, who denounced globalization in similar terms. Under such circumstance, Montebourg argued, a policy of "competitiveness" inflicted on French workers was pure deception. French workers were already very productive by international standards. They could not compete with Chinese or Bangladeshi workers nor should they be expected to try to do so. Closer to home Montebourg criticized the Germans along with the Chinese: Mrs. Merkel, too, pursued a policy of pure selfishness, refusing to raise salaries and internal consumption, a policy desperately needed to restore trade balances within the EU. Germany had to stimulate imports, not aggressively export while the euro was valued above its proper level. Montebourg condemned the German lecturing of the Greeks: Greek debt, he said, was a drop of water in a vast ocean of trillions of dollars of international bailouts of banks in the United States and Europe.

Austerity is not necessarily exclusively about trimming the welfare state, although a consensus appears to exist in Europe and America that the levels the welfare state has achieved are unsustainable in the face of an aging population with a smaller number of workers able to support

DOI: 10.1057/9781137356918.0007

the growing numbers of retirees. In France, where there is a much more vigorous tradition of overt social protest than in Germany, the government has more typically been forced to retreat in the face of popular protest, as during the strikes of 1995. Austerity has a long history. Its virtues were preached by Calvinists and the Scotch economists of the 18th century who praised parsimony and thrift. It appeals to the semi-religious idea of salvation through suffering: there is virtue and the promise of redemption through pain. It suggests itself in the same way that a medical patient might choose the most extreme and painful treatment in the hope, against evidence, that it will provide more chance of a cure.

But the most extraordinary thing about the revival of austerity in the current political climate is that its practitioners seem unaware that it defies one of the most obvious of historical lessons: it was used and abused in the early years of the depression in Germany before Hitler and in the United States before Roosevelt with similar disastrous effects on the economy in both nations, and in Germany, on politics. Austerity in Germany, not inflation, led to the rise of Hitler. In today's Europe austerity and unemployment are again feeding the resurgence of the extreme Right.

Hollande's campaign was premised on a modification of the austerity policy so as to permit or encourage a modicum of growth, but he did not go so far as to propose the policy's elimination. Hollande did propose the establishment of Eurobonds, financial instruments sold with the full faith and backing of the entire European Union, to finance a remedy for the debt crisis, and he called for the existing debt to be mutualized, pooled together, and centralized, to be paid by the EU. He vigorously supported monetarization of the debt, a policy pursued by Mario Draghi at the European Central Bank, who had vowed to do what he could to save the euro. Draghi as earlier noted made hundreds of billions of euros available to the banks at 1% interest, allowing them to use the funds to buy Greek debt at the reduced rate of 5% and still make a hefty profit. This policy helped the banks and paralleled Ben Bernanke's policy of "quantitative easing" in the United States, but it was not identical to Bernanke's policy and was much more limited. Merkel allowed Draghi to pursue this policy without open protest, but she drew the line at collectivization of the debt through Eurobonds along the lines that Hollande proposed. To accept that was too obviously to shift recovery costs onto the backs of German taxpayers, which Merkel would not do although the Nordic

DOI: 10.1057/9781137356918.0007

countries and Germany have benefited from artificially low interest rates on their debts.

Interest rates on the French debt were at historic lows as well in 2012, yet pessimistic prognostications continued to be made about the French economy and its prospects. Merkel steadfastly refused to consider a hardy policy of rescue for the euro, however, and Hollande's call for Eurobonds during his campaign was slapped down by the German government. Merkel rejected any proposed remedy that would require the German taxpayer to pay anything to alleviate the crisis, nor did she allow any default to imperil the German banks, however improvident their loans might have been. Sarkozy cooperated quietly in the implementation of this policy. Hollande raised questions about it but he decided to cooperate in the end as well. Another bizarre feature of the euro crisis lay in its appeal to national stereotypes if not racist ones: Germans railed against lazy Greeks who allegedly refused to work or pay taxes, and who were said to quit their otherwise easy government jobs every day at 3 p.m.

The euro crisis has had a huge social cost, however, as parties of the radical Right and Left have arisen and flourished in response to the crisis. Greece also has a dynamic new party of the Left, Syriza, with which Mélenchon has allied his Front de Gauche, in an attempt to establish a united front of the Left in Europe against austerity. Much more ominously a fascist party, Golden Dawn, has taken root in Greece as well. The National Front in France eschews any suggestion of fascist-like violence, but it flourishes as the depression intensifies and resulting unemployment is prolonged. Marine Le Pen actively sought Europe-wide cooperation for the establishment of an anti-European movement to contest the elections for the European parliament scheduled in 2014. The European elections of May 2014 brought anti-Europe deputies into the European parliament where they now number 25% of the total.

Clearly, what was needed as outcome of the change of administration in Paris was a new course or direction for the EU as a whole that under normal circumstances France should have been able to accomplish. But it appeared early and became more and more pronounced as the French election process unfolded that such change was in no way likely to become part of the election's outcome. A new government there would be, yes. But there would be no change in European policy other than a token allocation from the European stabilization fund toward investment in growth: a total of 130 billion euros to be spread over 17 countries in the Eurozone. There would be no American-like stimulus,

DOI: 10.1057/9781137356918.0007

which economists in the United States like Paul Krugman still criticized as insufficient to bring the country out of the depression, although it prevented the severity of the crisis in America being experienced on the level currently felt in Europe.

Hollande was under pressure to adopt a more radical position during his campaign. The Socialist party has a battery of academic economists who sympathize with it. No less than 42 prestigious economists signed a manifesto calling for the election of François Hollande, which was published in *Le Monde* on April 17, 2012.[12] They called for reconsideration of the EU austerity policy, which inhibited growth, and a reorientation of the EU's structure. The stability pact must be accompanied by an agreement to implement a policy of growth. The manifesto condemned Sarkozy for a blunt and foolish policy of simply replacing every two government workers who left or retired with a single hire— this being the means the Sarkozy government used to attack what many regarded as a bloated government bureaucracy. The economists further demanded an aggressive policy with regard to youth employment and the separation by law of savings banks from financial speculation markets. They insisted on a progressive taxation policy infused with concern for social justice and the elimination of tax evasion and "off-shore" tax shelters, whether in the Channel Islands or the Caribbean. And they went on to question the consumer society itself: was France to be a society of planned obsolescence and resulting waste and pollution, or a society with heavy public investment in health, education, and improved environment and quality of life?

This was all very well. But the same economists went on to endorse, indeed certify Hollande's promise of budgetary constraint. All their recommendations were pronounced to be consistent with a five-year plan of bringing the French budget into balance. This objective was a far cry from the earlier period during the Socialist primary, when some of the same economists pressured Hollande from the Left, fearing that his proposals were not up to the task of bringing about growth even were they fully to be adopted. Hollande was critical, to be sure, of the policies of Sarkozy and his prime minister, François Fillon, but Hollande was also reluctant to advocate positive alternatives lest he be accused of laxity with regard to fiscal matters. The Socialist economists demanded that more aggressive policies from the Left be clearly articulated by their putative leader.[13]

Another political football was France's loss of its AAA credit rating on its bonds in the estimation of the financial triumvirate of Fitch,

Moody, and Standard and Poor's, for which Sarkozy took the blame. Of course the United States and France had both lost their AAA ratings, and neither economy had any difficulty borrowing just the same. The rating agencies, moreover, are the same ones that falsified the ratings of the securitized mortgages in the United States, giving the risky securities AAA ratings and thus helping to defraud investors who purchased them. Moreover low interest rates prevailing in the United States and France on government bonds made the debt much less a matter of genuine economic concern, as Paul Krugman argued again and again. But traditional thinking prevailed throughout the political spectrum, with the exception of the moderate Left of Montebourg or the far Left of Mélenchon, to whom few "serious" politicians listened.

Globalization was a campaign issue as well as the euro crisis; in fact the two were paired together, the EU being seen as an agent of globalization. In France, like elsewhere in the industrial West, the manufacturing economy has declined and cheap consumer goods are now for the most party manufactured in Asia. The industrial production sector of the French economy declined in the ten years from 2002 to 2012 from 26% to 18% of the national economy, according to the World Fact Book published by the CIA. In Germany the decline was slight by comparison, from 31% to 28%. The closure of factories in France was frequently the object of protests by the workers affected amid calls for government intervention. These were the years of the Chirac and Sarkozy presidencies, and Sarkozy could be blamed as having been finance minister under Chirac before he became president of the Republic. There were during the campaign calls to "*reterritorialiser*" the French economy, bring industry back home from abroad. Even François Bayrou, the Centrist candidate, thundered that "France is dying because it is no longer able to produce what it needs to live."[14]

Hollande made a personal visit during his campaign to Florange, a major French steel installation near Metz, where the steel manufacturer ArcinorMittal, owned by the Indian steel magnate Lakshmi Mittal, was in process of closing the blast furnaces putting hundreds of workers out of their jobs. The workers were demonstrating on a site that symbolized France's plight; the closure would mean a further step in the country's "de-industrialization" and was being decided in large part by Mittal, who resides in England, but bought much of the declining European steel industry to incorporate it into his world steel empire. Hollande denounced Mittal as a financier as opposed to an industrialist

DOI: 10.1057/9781137356918.0007

(a distinction without a difference) and argued that the mill was profit-able. Its closure, Hollande argued, was part of a global plan by Mittal to concentrate steel production in Asia rather than to divest the firm of an unprofitable enterprise. Hollande promised a law preventing factory closures in France unless the enterprise was put up for sale first and failed to find a buyer.

The issue returned to plague Hollande after he became president, however. Mittal insisted he must close the blast furnaces at Florange; better and more modern ones were meeting the needs of a declining market for finished steel at Dunkirk and Fos, both on the coast where raw materials were more easily delivered. Hollande talked of French government nationalization of the furnaces at Florange if Mittal refused to sell or was unable to find a buyer, but the French government in the end was reluctant to take such a step; it could hardly commit to so costly a measure while trying to trim its budget to meet the commitment to the European stability pact. Hollande instead negotiated a settlement that allowed Mittal to close the blast furnaces but committed him to continue finishing steel at Florange. Workers would not be fired but those in excess at the site could transfer elsewhere or gradually retire without replacement. But the lesson of Florange appeared to be that the de-industrialization of France was ineluctable.[15]

Nor did the leading French economists of Socialist bent provide much of an alternative. It is instructive to peruse their texts, published in an effort to explain the economic crisis that hit France in 2008. Philippe Aghion, for example, is a Harvard economist half the year and the rest of the time a presence in France; his books are published in both languages but he has no hesitation contributing to *La Revue Socialiste*, the official publication of the PS.[16] Aghion is not a Keynesian. Keynes was appropriate to what he calls a "Fordist" economy. The term "Fordism" denotes the rapid industrializing "catch-up" economy of the postwar years, when growth rates of 6 or even 8% were common, the period from 1945 to 1975 that the French commonly refer to as "*les Trentes Glorieuses.*" France has moved into a post-industrial service economy since then. This is not to say that the Sarkozy administration did well to allow the levels of de-industrialization experienced by France in the first decade of the 21st century. Still it is the classical industrial economy that has declined. The fault, says Aghion, was in allowing the educational establishment to deteriorate which in turn stifled the kind of innovation necessary for growth. Growth in the new economy comes not through "catch-up";

DOI: 10.1057/9781137356918.0007

France has caught up and falls among the major world economies anywhere from fifth to eighth in the world ranking of GDP and national income. Growth in the new world economy comes through innovation. To accomplish it does not mean to rely on the private sector, for Aghion however. It is rather necessary to rethink the state.[17]

France excels in its health system which is the best in the world; it must build on health as a major area of innovation and production. France must also encourage startups: French economists turn with a wistful eye to Silicon Valley and San Francisco in sunny California. To accomplish that it correspondingly will be necessary to invest heavily in education, so as to train the specialists needed to increase the Research and Development budget in order to make the country first class. And finally, France must pursue not a politics of consumer demand, the Keynesian way, but rather a policy of emphasis on supply-side economics. Aghion says he is not proposing neo-liberalism, however; rather he wants a revived policy of targeted sectors of the economy where France is already strong in which the state can invest and encourage innovation through a new industrial policy. And additionally, Aghion notes that France must pursue actively a policy of encouraging immigrants. Over the long term its aging population will require more and younger workers than the existing birthrate provides to support its economy. Aghion wants selective immigration, however, noting the contribution of immigrants to the high number of startups in America.

Daniel Cohen and Philippe Ashkenazy are also known as progressive economists. In an extended essay titled *"Le mal français"* they appear not to address economics or politics as the source of France's problems; rather, incivility and lack of trust among the French population.[18] The French do not trust their neighbors or believe in one another's honesty; their society functions like a zero-sum game in which gain for one's self equals loss for another. They are neither public spirited nor honest; if they happen upon found money they will keep it, and if they find a way to cheat on taxes and can get away with it they will do so. This, Cohen and Ashkenazy tell us, is not the case in the Scandinavian countries and Germany, where economic growth and prosperity reign along with civic-mindedness and trust.

It was once so in France as well, they argue. France's negative traits are a product of the Vichy regime, the German occupation, and legacy of corporatism left by those experiences: on the one hand there is excessive centralization, and on the other a system of class differentiation in

DOI: 10.1057/9781137356918.0007

education and inequality of opportunity. The result may be seen in the unhappy state of labor relations in France; the nation is mired in class conflict that has elsewhere been transcended and that hampers production in France through excessive strikes and conflicts. Unionization in France, once at 18% of the labor force, has declined to 8%. In Scandinavia and Germany it is more like 70% among industrial workers and unions represent their workers in conferences with management, structuring salaries and benefits through mutual bargaining, not by means of state regulation and bureaucratic enforcement as is the case in France. In France conflict-laden social relations prevail, not social dialogue, with the result that the economy suffers.

The economists offer as a cure for the French a policy of "flexicurity" (sometimes spelled "flexisecurity"). This is an innovative model of labor practice pioneered by the Danes and currently under active discussion everywhere in the EU. It is characterized by very lax government regulation of employment and dismissal by management, in short flexibility in the use of labor as needed. This is the opposite of the situation in France where the state closely regulates hiring and firing and the conditions for each, inhibiting employers from hiring for fear of being stuck with workers they may not need at a later time and high associated labor costs for the extensive social benefits they receive. Flexicurity also means a policy of state support for labor, security for workers in which the state, not employers, is responsible for social benefits, and more importantly, absolute security is guaranteed for workers who are unemployed. Flexicurity must be accompanied also by universality and fairness in distribution of benefits by the state. The French system, say Ashkenazy and Cohen is characterized by statist corporatism in the distribution of social benefits; elites and the privileged get special treatment. The French lack confidence that their benefits are fairly and equally distributed. The economists insist there is a positive correlation and causative effect between flexicurity, fair distributive polices, and economic growth. They also extend their model of chronic incivility and lack of trust to the corresponding political crisis; the French also believe their politicians are hopelessly corrupt and must be so to succeed. They consequently have little faith that any new government will either keep its promises or provide a remedy for what ails the nation.

Jean-Hervé Lorenzi also enjoys a reputation as a Left-leaning economist who actively supported Hollande. Lorenzi, in his own contribution to an analysis of the impact of the world economic crisis

DOI: 10.1057/9781137356918.0007

in France, castigates what he terms the manic obsession with decline of the French. Of course this is nothing new; the French through their history have had their Cassandras predicting demographic and other forms of disaster. Books like the best-selling Nicolas Bavarez's *La France qui tombent* have appeared in every generation.[19] The French have lost faith in public authority and correspondingly distrust the wider move toward European integration. Instead the desire for retreat to some sort of protectionist fortress attracts more and more voters. Lorenzi does insist that France look inward for remedies. The French are not Germans and they cannot adopt the German model. Lorenzi wants the French to focus on their own successes: the nation boasts leaders among the major world multinationals such as Vuitton in luxury goods, Airbus Group in aviation, Parisbas in banking, and Areva in nuclear energy. France has the highest birthrate in Europe, near replacement level (2.1) although the nation will still need immigrants in the future. French workers are among the world's most productive and the country has the best health system in the world.[20] One danger sign is the deterioration in the nation's education system; the country's research and development budget needs to be aggressively expanded. But the nation's culture is thriving and its film industry world class—an answer perhaps to an American writer for *Time magazine* who published a widely controversial long essay in November 2007 titled "The Death of French Culture."[21] Moreover, notes Lorenzi, despite an obsessive pessimism, the overwhelming majority are in fact happy with their lot.

Lorenzi lays out a firmly social-democratic solution to the crisis. The enemy is finance capitalism, whose prescriptions involve protection against inflation and "malign neglect of unemployment." Finance capitalism has ushered in a new world of inequality even as it functions as a world unto itself, with detrimental effects on the real economy. The remedies for this situation involve the revival of the state. The state must take control of the banks, if necessary nationalize them, and see to it that interest rates are lowered almost to zero. The state, or the EU, must guarantee deposits, regulate and revive the real estate and automobile sectors of the economy, and most importantly undertake programs involving massive new expenditure and strong deficits as long as necessary to end the crisis. The power of finance capital must be tamed and the hedge funds controlled along with the investment banks, while off-shore tax shelters are eliminated along with golden parachutes and the obscene power of the rating agencies.[22]

DOI: 10.1057/9781137356918.0007

One dare not conclude a survey of France's progressive economists without attention to their most recent media star, Thomas Piketty, whose *Capital in the Twenty-First Century* was greeted by Paul Krugman as the outstanding study of its kind of the year if not the decade.[23] Piketty wears his partisanship on his sleeve; he was the founding director of France's School of Economics but quickly resigned to immerse himself in Ségolène Royal's campaign. Piketty's concern is what appears to have become the structural inequality inherent in contemporary capitalism, which in the absence of sufficient growth he fears in the future will become unsustainable. He notes the rising ratio of capital to labor in national income and wealth in the richest capitalist nations, and the copious profits reaped by businesses in a period of near-zero growth and stagnant if not declining wages. His conclusions cause one to at least wonder whether the EU's current austerity is not designed to achieve that result: high profits, low wages, and high unemployment which helps keep labor costs low and discourages immigration. Piketty has offered proposals for tax reform to mitigate inequality, but despairs of the capacity of democratic regimes to implement them. Not surprisingly, after supporting the election of François Hollande, it did not take him long to denounce the people who govern France as "nullities."[24]

Piketty notwithstanding, the absence of trenchant analysis of the European Union and the euro in these works is striking; the socialists, like the UMP in France, share the consensus about Europe's necessity for balanced budgets and belt-tightening, and they do not speculate about how to force more growth-oriented policies upon their recalcitrant European partners. They seem to share the national obsession with competitiveness, ignoring Montebourg's prescient warning that French workers cannot and should not be made to compete with Chinese or Bangladeshi workers. The more cynical might note that some of them, like their American counterparts, have financial and corporate ties and emoluments.[25] Their remedies do provide for an activist state, targeting and promoting industrial sectors, and improving the workings of the welfare state, but innovations like flexicurity sound like concessions to management permitting it to control labor costs by hiring and firing without regulation and with impunity. One of Hollande's ministers referred to the term "flexisecurity" as an "aberrant oxymoron." The word was absent in Hollande's campaign literature and rhetoric but later surfaced with proposals for his employment pact with management. And seeking to alleviate France's alleged incivility and distrust

DOI: 10.1057/9781137356918.0007

is hardly an objective that Hollande could profitably pursue even if he were guaranteed two terms and not one, in an era in which a single term like that of Sarkozy promises to become the rule. Hollande promised to reverse the trend toward increasing unemployment by the end of 2014. His economists with a few exceptions did not offer him a means of doing so. Nor were his campaign promises adequate to the task.

Notes

1   Thomas Piketty, *Capital in the Twenty-First Century* (Cambridge: Harvard University Press, 2014).

2   Charles Mayer, *In Search of Stability: Explorations in Historical Political Economy* (Cambridge: Cambridge University Press, 1987).

3   Perry Anderson, *The New Old World* (London: Verso Books, 2011).

4   John Gillingham, *European Integration, 1950–2003: Superstate or New Market Economy?* (Cambridge: Cambridge University Press, 2003).

5   The works of Alan Milward and Andrew Moravscik are germane here.

6   Bernard Moss, *Monetary Union in Crisis: The European Union as a Neo-Liberal Construction* (New York: Palgrave Macmillan, 2005).

7   *Le Monde,* April 10, 2013.

8   Alan Bergounioux, personal interview, June 17, 2013.

9   Marc Blythe, *Austerity: The History of a Dangerous Idea* (Oxford: Oxford University Press, 2013).

10   See Phillip Arestis and Malcolm Sawyer, *The Euro Crisis* (New York: Palgrave Macmillan, 2012).

11   *The Economist,* May 26, 2012.

12   *L'Express,* May 17, 2012; *Le Monde,* May 17, 2012.

13   Sylvia Zappi, «Les economists de gauche poussent François Hollande à se démarquer de la politique d'austerité», *Le Monde,* November 9, 2011.

14   Jean-Luc Mano, *Les Phrases chocs de la campagne présidentielle* (Paris: Jean-Claude Gawsewitch, 2012), p. 38.

15   See Laurent Binet, *Rien ne se passe comme prévu* (Paris: Grasset, 2012) on Hollande's campaign promises at Florange; also *Le Monde,* October 2, 2013, and February 23, 2014, on how the crisis played out.

16   Philippe Aghion, «Comment redresser l'économie française,» *La Revue Socialiste* (45–46, 2011).

17   Philippe Aghion and Alexandre Roulet, *Repenser l'Etat : Pour une socialedémocratie de l'innovation* (Paris: Seuil, 2011).

18   In Philippe Askenazy and Daniel Cohen, *16 Nouvelles questions d'economie* (Paris: Albin Michel, 2010).

19 Nicolas Bavarez, *La France qui tombe : Un constat clinique du déclin français* (Paris: Perrin, 2003). Bavarez, a conservative, indicts a top-heavy state as the cause of Franc's alleged decline.

20 Jean-Hervé Lorenzi, *La Fabuleuse destin d'une puissance intermédiaire* (Paris: Grasset, 2011).

21 Later published as a book, Donald Morrison and Antoine Compagnon, *The Death of French Culture* (New York: Polity Press, 2010).

22 Pierre Dockès and Jean-Hervé Lorenzi, *Fin de Monde ou sortie de crise* (Paris: Perrin, 2009), pp. 54–58. A collection of essays by members of the *Cercle des économistes*, most of whom offer bold policies opposite of those which Hollande would appear to have chosen.

23 Piketty, *Capital in the Twenty-First Century*. "Wealth over Work," *The New York Times*, March 23, 2014.

24 Europe 1, *Le Lab Politique*, September 8, 2012.

25 "Les économists à gages sur la salette," *Le Monde Diplomatique*, March 2012. The article notes revelations in the United States of Lawrence Summers's earnings from the world of finance and the film *Inside Job*. Lorenzi in particular maintains ties with real estate and insurance interests while serving as president of the influential *Circle des economists* and counselor to François Hollande.

DOI: 10.1057/9781137356918.0007

5
The French Elections Decoded

Abstract: *The legislative elections, held on June 10 and June 17, 2012, demonstrated clearly the distortions and inadequacies of the French political system. The participation rate was the lowest ever. The Socialists and their allies, totaling a minority of 43% of the electorate, were assured nevertheless of a huge majority in the National Assembly on the second ballot. Neither the National Front nor the Center could win more than three and two seats, respectively, despite the high showings of their presidential candidates a month earlier. Hollande seemed dynamic and popular at the outset of his presidency and appointed a government equally representative of men and women. But he showed he could not prevent the mixing of the personal and the political and quickly revealed himself bereft of choices in terms of reviving the economy. France appeared a no-choice democracy in the midst of a severe political crisis.*

Wall, Irwin. *France Votes: The Election of François Hollande.* New York: Palgrave Macmillan, 2014. doi: 10.1057/9781137356918.0008.

DOI: 10.1057/9781137356918.0008

The election results on the first ballot placed the candidates in the order expected: Hollande's first place finish, however, marked the first time that a challenger gained more votes than the incumbent on the first ballot since 1958. French law does not permit the results of exit polls to be revealed before the closing of the polls at 8 p.m. on election day, but voters picked up indications on the internet through euphemisms: Flanby according to one report was said to be selling better than goulash. Hollande received 28.63% to Sarkozy's 27.18%. Marine Le Pen came in third place with 17.9%; she easily met the challenge presented by Mélenchon who finished fourth with 11.1%. Bayrou came in fifth with 9.13% and Eva Joly sixth with the very low figure of 2.31%.

There was surprise in these totals: the high total gained by Marine Le Pen was a shock for journalists and much of the public; and although Mélenchon's total was lower than expected, 11.1% was higher than the Communists or any other "Left of the Left" party had received in recent elections going back to 1981 and represented a serious challenge to Hollande's Socialist party. Bayrou and Joly's disappointing results showed the near-collapse of Centrism and Ecology as political platforms. Bayrou had received 18.57% of the vote in 2007. The Ecologist vote had been insignificant in 2007, but the party made a comeback in 2009 as part of a coalition under Daniel Cohn-Bendit in the European elections of that year, winning 8 deputies and 14% of the vote in the European elections. Following the 2012 French elections, however, it appeared that neither ecologist party had a future. The remaining candidates all received less than 2% of the vote. The polls were extremely accurate with regard to Hollande and Sarkozy on the first ballot, off by 1% in the case of Hollande and only 0.5% in the case of Sarkozy. But they underestimated the Le Pen vote by 4.5% and overestimated Mélenchon's total by 2%. The National Front continued to defy the pollsters, who underestimated it by 4% in 2002 also, and overestimated it by the same 4% in 2007. The polls did not show in 2007 that Sarkozy would manage to steal a good part of the FN's electorate, and they could not predict that he would so dramatically fail to do so in 2012. Le Pen voters appear not to want to cooperate with pollsters.

In any French presidential election the Left faces a daunting challenge on the second ballot. Despite a glorious and dramatic history in the country from the perspective of its adherents, who claim the Great Revolution of 1789 and the subsequent revolutions of the 19th century in 1830, 1848, and 1870 as their own, the Left has governed seldom, and

DOI: 10.1057/9781137356918.0008

the natural penchant of the electorate is to the Right. There were only two Socialist-led governments during the entire history of the Third and Fourth Republics from 1870 to 1958: the Popular Front government of 1936–1937 and the so-called Republican Front government of Guy Mollet from January 1956 to May 1957. The Pierre Mendès France interlude in 1954–1955 was progressive by any standard, but Mendès France was not then a Socialist, and even when he later claimed to have become one he was never a Marxist. The definitive arrival of the Socialists as a government party only happened in 1981 with the presidency of François Mitterrand, who governed for two terms, from 1981 to 1995. François Hollande is only the second Socialist president of France in the entire history of the country.

Moreover, the total vote of the parties of the Left on the first ballot of the 2012 elections came to 43.6% of the electorate. This was hardly the best the Left had ever done either: in 1981, before Mitterrand's victory, the total Left vote was 48.5%, an all-time high, but still leaving the Left a minority in the country. Polls in 2012 demonstrate the continued right-ist leanings of the French electorate: 62% said that there are too many immigrants in France, 60% regarded Islam as a menace to Western Civilization, 51% believed that unemployed workers could find work if they really tried, and a plurality of 43% favored economic protectionism, while only 23% wanted an economy open to the world. The rest had no opinion. Many of Le Pen's views are widely shared outside her party.

If history is any guide, however, Hollande had the requisite minimum of 43% Left vote that he needed for him to win on the second ballot. He needed to expand his base, and in effect he did so, garnering another 8 million votes to carry him to his final total on the second ballot of 51.4%. He got these votes from those voters who on the first ballot had voted either for Bayrou or Le Pen, or who had abstained. In fact the polls showed that he received 35% of the Le Pen vote and 40% of the Bayrou vote. But he did not have a mandate to govern from the Left in any sense. The election was more a referendum on Sarkozy than a vote for Hollande; Sarkozy lost more than Hollande won.[1]

To general surprise the actual margin on May 6 was also much narrower than expected. French law prohibits the publication of polls during the week before an election. The last minute closing of the gap between the candidates went undetected and while the finish was not razor thin, neither did Hollande win the overwhelming mandate he had hoped for. The final score of 51.4% to 48.6% was respectable at best for

DOI: 10.1057/9781137356918.0008

either candidate, but a disappointment for Hollande if not a solace to Sarkozy, and a reminder that polls, if they are accurate, are glimpses of the moment that fail to capture the evolution of opinion going forward.

Two elements that played out in the final week eluded observers: the dynamism of Sarkozy and the almost placid and misplaced confidence of his opponent. Sarkozy was not the "normal" candidate but the times did not call for Hollande's bland assertions of normality either. Sarkozy's almost explicit racism in his appeal to Le Pen's voters may well have attracted more of them than he lost among Centrists. Sarkozy nevertheless tried to garner the Le Pen vote on the second ballot as he had done in the past, shamelessly attacking the Roma in France. He held his own demonstration in opposition to the Left's May Day in which he celebrated what he called "real" Labor, that of laborers who are exposed to the elements, who suffer, and who do not want shirkers to receive higher wages than them. He did not indicate what kind of work or workers qualified as "unreal," or false, however. Le Pen, despite receiving her brevet of republicanism from the desperate president, however, declined to endorse him in turn. She persisted in tying together the UMP and PS into a single corrupt amalgam she called the UMPS. Bayrou declined to endorse Sarkozy as he had done in 2007. While not telling his followers how to vote, he personally endorsed Hollande, obviously repelled by Sarkozy's rhetoric. In fact Sarkozy got no endorsements, while Mélenchon, Bayrou, Joly, and two splinter Left candidates all supported Hollande.

Hollande perhaps saved himself from defeat by managing a spirited television debate held between the ballots; Sarkozy had demanded several debates between the two final contenders, but Hollande limited it to the traditional one debate, which he handled almost ingeniously. He attacked Sarkozy's celebration of "real" workers and said he did not distinguish between real and unreal or false labor; he did not distinguish, as Sarkozy did, between those unions who pleased him and those that did not. In a lengthy response to a general question about what he would do as president, Hollande intoned the phrase "Moi, président de la République," leaving the conditionality of the assertion to the listener to infer, and habituating him/her at the same time to the idea that Hollande might in fact the next week become president. Subsequently it seemed a brilliant and carefully planned stratagem; but Laurent Binet, who witnessed Hollande's rather chaotic rehearsal-preparations for the debate, had not seen it rehearsed, and so asked Hollande where he had

DOI: 10.1057/9781137356918.0008

gotten it. Hollande said it came to him during the debate itself, prompted by a question that began, "Vous, président de la Répulique," to which Hollande simply replied in kind, "Moi, président de la République."[2] Sarkozy lacked the presence of mind to remind Hollande that he was not yet president and would not be until the votes were counted, if then.

But Sarkozy scored some points too; the debate may have been a victory for Hollande but it was not a rout. Sarkozy sarcastically remarked that Hollande's "normal" presidency could not be up to the level of the challenges facing the nation. Calling attention to Hollande's desire to tax the rich, Sarkozy said the difference between them was that "you (Hollande) want fewer rich people; I want fewer poor people."

But as Sarkozy's immigrant baiting and appeal to the National Front voters showed, his campaigning theme was not about economics, unless meant to imply that immigrants were the cause of the unemployment after all. Sarkozy rhetorically ran to defend eternal France, to protect its identity and the sanctity of its frontiers, in the name of the Nation. Hollande ran for inclusion rather than exclusion, openness rather than a closed society, in defense of the Republic rather than the Nation. But all this would be quickly forgotten once the election was over.[3]

There was only a week's interval between the election and the passing of power ceremony at the Elysée palace. Hollande used the time to appoint a prime minister and put together his government. He ignored Martine Aubry's candidacy for prime minister, turning to the popular president of the socialist group in the National Assembly and mayor of Nantes, Jean-Marc Ayrault. He put Laurent Fabius, one-time prime minister and one of the power Socialist "elephants" into office as minister of foreign affairs. His Socialist opponents in the primary election who had rallied to his support, Manuel Valls and Arnaud de Montebourg, received the Ministries of the Interior and Industrial Production. Pierre Moscovici, a long-time Socialist and ally, became minister of finance. There were 34 ministers, 17 male and 17 female, but wags noticed the absence of women in any of the "key" ministries, the Interior, Foreign Affairs, and Finance. This created a rather bizarre parallel to de Gaulle, who formed his government after the war and included the Communist party but pointedly refused them any of these key ministries, suggesting their ineligibility in terms of worthiness or patriotism. Hollande surely meant no such thing, but the omission remains.

Once elected and inaugurated, Hollande hit the ground running. It is a singular advantage to a newly elected president in France that allows

DOI: 10.1057/9781137356918.0008

him to appoint a government immediately upon taking office, and hence able to act before gaining a vote of confidence in the yet to be elected National Assembly. Hollande immediately set out for Berlin, being forced to return to Paris in flight, however, and to start out again after his plane was hit by lightning en route. He dominated the conversation in the German capitol, hardly letting Merkel speak as he insisted on the necessity for Eurobonds as a solution to the Greek crisis and a broader policy of economic growth for the EU. This brought a none-too polite refusal by the Germans, but Hollande appeared to signal a profound shift in the nature of the Franco-German tandem that has in the past governed the evolution of the EU, scattering the marbles so to speak, and bringing the Italians and Spaniards into a kind of directorate as major players. Mrs. Merkel was made to feel the pressure of the need for growth policies and the reaction against austerity, even if she did not bend to it.

Hollande went to the United States where he announced French troops would be removed from Afghanistan by the end of 2012, an early campaign promise. He went to Afghanistan to visit his troops. After that he went to Russia where he failed to win Putin over to the campaign to remove Assad in Syria. All this, of course, with an eye on the legislative elections scheduled on June 10 and 17, in which Hollande hoped to win a large "presidential" majority for his Socialist party.

Hollande appointed his prime minister and his cabinet immediately after his election, as French procedure allows. The government, headed by Jean-Marc Ayrault, the former mayor of Nantes, swung into action at once, needing to win a majority in the impending legislative elections on June 10. The justice minister, a black member of parliament from Guiana named Christiane Taubira, eliminated juvenile tribunals, courts created by Sarkozy that were authorized to try juveniles as adults. This was viciously attacked by the Right, without effect. The education minister, Vincent Peillon, announced university reform, promising more autonomy to individual campuses. The housing minister, Cécile Duflot, announced a rent freeze, pending legislation to resolve the housing crisis. A few days before the first ballot Ayrault's government announced the fulfillment of another Hollande campaign promise, a return to retirement at age 60 for certain categories of workers, in particular those who started work at age 18 or lower and who had made payments to the retirement system for 41 or more years. Some 100,000 were affected, at a cost of over one billion euros the first year, to be financed by a slight increase in the social security tax. *Le Figaro* at once denounced the reform

DOI: 10.1057/9781137356918.0008

as running counter to the European orthodoxy of austerity. But that was its point: the inclusion of these workers under Sarkozy's original plan to increase the retirement age to 62 was perceived as a particular injustice by the French.[4] But so was austerity generally seen as an injustice in Europe, argued the Socialists, in which it appeared that the poor are being made to pay for an economic crisis launched by the imprudence if not stupidity of financiers and bankers and the laxity of politicians.

The polls showed widespread support for the new president's initial package of measures. No less than 88% favored retirement at 60 for workers who had begun in their teens and worked 40 years. The French supported Hollande's other changes with less but still overwhelming enthusiasm: 69% favored heavy taxes on the rich, with a 75% tax rate on incomes over one million euros per year; 75% of Left voters backed the tax along with 65% of Le Pen voters and 49% of Sarkozy voters favorable to taxing the rich as well.

Delineating Right and Left in French politics was becoming increasingly difficult. Hollande enjoyed similarly large majorities in favor of new jobs promised in education, an end to cuts in hiring new government workers, and legalizing gay marriage. Yet despite this the new president enjoyed only 55% personal popularity two weeks into his administration, a figure well below the initial favorable ratings of previous presidents including his three predecessors, Mitterrand, Chirac, and Sarkozy. Moreover, voters remained skeptical of what the new president could accomplish: they appeared to respect his honesty and sincerity, but they thought he lacked the stature and dynamism of his disliked predecessor. A huge majority of the French believed that conditions would be worse for their children than they were at the time of the elections, and half feared for their jobs as unemployment mounted. Large pluralities believed the president powerless to effect real change for the better.[5]

French pessimism seemed a national characteristic, to be sure. An international Gallup poll showed the French to be the most pessimistic of peoples in the world, the most pessimistic among 51 nations polled, coming in last just behind Afghanistan and Iraq.[6] Observers were quick to note the high standard of living in France, the longevity of its population, the excellence of its medical care, and its central place as a destination of the world's tourists. There should be no cause for that level of pessimism in a country so naturally rich and well-endowed. No matter, the French seemed to fear the worst.

DOI: 10.1057/9781137356918.0008

The polls in the week before the legislative balloting on June 10 showed the electorate more evenly divided than the presidential election indicated, although Hollande's victory margin of only slightly more than 2% had been in itself disappointing. In the first ballot voting for the National Assembly the two major parties each did slightly better than their presidential candidates, but still revealed themselves to be minorities of the electorate. The PS in fact did not even crack the barrier of 30% while the UMP languished near 27%. However, the National Front and Front de Gauche totals fell off significantly more, as these voters likely stayed home, or decided to cast their ballots for the larger parties closest to their views. The PS and its allies (Ecologists and Left Radicals) taken together received about 43% of the vote on the first ballot while the UMP got 35%. The remainder of the vote was scattered among the smaller parties.

It was clear, however, that a solid Socialist majority would emerge from the second ballot on June 17, in which the two or three leading candidates in the electoral districts squared off against each other. The absence of their leaders—Bayrou, Le Pen, and Mélenchon were all eliminated on the first ballot—and the smaller electorate badly hurt the smaller parties, few of whose candidates survived to the second round. The National Front declined to 13.6% of the vote and the Front de Gauche fell to about 7%, with the Center almost wiped out, coming in at 2%. As in the presidential elections the month before, National Front voters would divide their votes between the two major parties on the second ballot, moreover, or worse for the UMP, field their own candidates, which was permitted in cases where they received 12.5% of the total of registered voters. This was a much higher bar than a percentage of those actually voting; the FN candidates actually needed 20% of those voting to stay in the race on the second ballot. Still, there were a significant number of "triangulaires," run-off races between three candidates, Socialist, UMP, and National Front, most of them working to the advantage of the Socialists since FN candidates drained away potential UMP votes.

A divided opposition meant that the Socialist plurality would translate into an even stronger presidential majority, the only remaining question being whether the majority would be a coalition dependent on FG or Ecologist deputies, or whether PS deputies would be numerous enough to rule by themselves. On June 17 the PS got a majority of 306 deputies out of 577, enough to rule by itself; with its allies it could count on 331 votes, or 341 votes for the government if the Front de Gauche were counted too. The UMP could count on 229 votes.

DOI: 10.1057/9781137356918.0008

The result revealed another paradox: all three dissident parties, which accounted for 38% of the voters on the first ballot of the presidential election, remain grossly under-represented in parliament. This could at least in part have been remedied by a return to a modified system of proportional representation, to which the PS was nominally committed. There are no signs that the party will make that reform a priority, however.

All the Socialist ministers in the newly formed government of Prime Minister Ayrault were either elected outright on the first ballot or well positioned ahead of their opponents and easily won on the second ballot. The prime minister led the pack, receiving 56% in his fief in Nantes. Hollande took clear satisfaction in the outcome. He had a mandate to carry out his policies, he said. But the political pundits seemed determined to find cause for lament, *Le Monde* leading the rest in deploring the large number of abstentions and the disappearance of the Center and relative collapse of the far Left.[7] One may wonder at this common French complaint. Is the center of the political spectrum necessarily the locus of truth? Is compromise, even if it could be achieved, necessarily a virtue? Pierre Mendès France famously said that "gouverner, c'est choisir" and wrote a book with that sobriquet as its title. Could one really counsel abstention in an election between Sarkozy and Hollande and claim superior discernment? Bayrou himself belied this by publicly endorsing Hollande on the second ballot of the presidential election after receiving less than 10% of the vote himself on the first. Sadly, he got no reward for doing so. He ran poorly in his own district, and the Socialist candidate refused to step down in his favor on the second ballot; there had been no prior agreement to do so but it would have been a nice gesture had the PS decided to do it even in the absence of a deal.

Jean-Luc Mélenchon meanwhile created something of a media sensation by choosing to run in the district of Pas-de-Calais near the Belgian border, more specifically in the town of Hénin-Baumont, targeting the former district where Marine Le Pen had chosen to run in 2007 and again in 2012. Mélenchon created a nostalgic symbolism: the coal-mining area had once been a Communist party stronghold but it now demonstrated, indeed dramatized, how former Communist voters had shifted from extremism of the Left to extremism of the Right. Mélenchon proposed to win these voters back to the Left, their historic home.

The Socialists gave him no quarter, however, putting up their own candidate against him on the first ballot. It appeared that Hollande was rather annoyed than pleased and would not have been happy if

DOI: 10.1057/9781137356918.0008

Mélenchon had won. Here was a second chance for the victorious Socialists to make a nice gesture to a potential political ally. As in the case of Bayrou, the party declined to do so, allowing Mélenchon to go down to defeat. The PS candidate came in narrowly ahead of Mélenchon, forcing him to quit the race, and then went on to defeat Marine Le Pen, but by a razor-thin difference of about 100 votes. It was a defeat that Marine Le Pen was able to trumpet as a major success, however, because her vote total increased by 10% over what it had been five years earlier. Hénin-Baumont went on to elect a National Front mayor in 2014.

Hollande's seemingly dynamic start of his presidency won him only a short proverbial honeymoon with the electorate, which the French call an *état de grâce*. The serenity and assurance of a calm and steady hand at the head of France, which he had appeared to establish in the first five weeks of his presidency, quickly began to collapse between ballots of the legislative elections. The "anti-Sarkozy," it seemed, would resemble his predecessor, one of whose most annoying characteristics had been to mix his public functions and his private life, divorcing and remarrying while occupying the Elysée and elevating the former model-turned-singer Carla Bruni to the newly baptized role of "Première Dame."

Ségolène Royal remained a force to contend with even after Hollande's elevation to the presidency. There remained a peculiar and potent symbolism in France's once-styled "Royal couple," even after their split, in their having succeeded one another as candidates for the presidency in 2007 and 2012. After his victory in the primary in October 2011, Hollande still thought he needed Royal's support to win the nomination and the presidency. He won her support by promising to support her candidacy for the presidency of the National Assembly in turn. Had she been elected she would have been the first woman to hold that post. Socialists saw this as fitting; others however disliked the idea of the president and his estranged former companion occupying the roles of president of the Republic and president of the National Assembly.

It was first necessary to assure Royal's election to the National Assembly, however, for which purpose she was "parachuted" into La Rochelle, a safe district in Southwestern coastal France that historically had always voted for the Left. The issue was complicated, however, by the resistance of the local Socialist candidate, Olivier Falorni, who violated party discipline, refused to step aside, and contested the seat against Royal on the first ballot. He lost, but he was almost her equal in popular support, receiving 28% of the vote against her 32%, and he got his 28% by

DOI: 10.1057/9781137356918.0008

reminding voters that he was the local boy and she an outsider. Falorni then refused calls for him to stand down in Royal's favor on the second ballot. Instead, the UMP candidate, assuming his own defeat in any case, stood down and mischievously threw his support to Falorni against Royal. Royal's presumably safe seat was now suddenly in danger in a run-off between two Socialists. President Hollande immediately declared his public support for Royal while the prime minster Ayrault and the Socialist party secretary Martine Aubry rushed down to La Rochelle to campaign for her.

Enter the new "Première Dame," the companion of the president of the last five years, Valérie Trierweiler, still of *Paris-Match*. Trierweiler had effortlessly stepped into her new role, accompanying the new president on his initial trips abroad and cozying up with foreign heads of state, including President Obama, meanwhile announcing, however, her intention to continue her career as journalist. As if to demonstrate her point, she consecrated her first article as first lady to a review of a new biography of Eleanor Roosevelt by Claude Katherine Kiejman, whose book highlighted the career as a journalist of the wife of Franklin Roosevelt. Trierweiler thought this a fitting example and model for herself as she carried out her public function as first lady alongside Francois Hollande from an office inside the Elysée. Like many journalists Trierweiler had a following on Twitter. She also had a turbulent history of involvement with the once "Royal" couple. The two powerful women in Hollande's life appeared to be publicly jealous of one another. When Hollande's second-ballot victory was celebrated in Tulle, Hollande's political base in the Corrèze, on May 6, the new president embraced Royal and kissed her on both cheeks in a show of public gratitude for her support. Trierweiler, as if to emphasize for television viewers the difference as the president embraced her in turn, made him kiss her on the lips. Innocent at the moment, it was an ominous precedent.[8]

The first lady's readers were surprised, shortly after Hollande's plea in favor of Royal's candidacy in La Rochelle, to find Valérie Trierweiler tweeting an endorsement of Royal's opponent, Falorni, who, she wrote, had earned the post of representative in the National Assembly by his many years of distinguished service to his fellow "Rochelais," of whom Royal was not one. Trierweiler did personally know and admire Falorni, who had previously himself been a loyal follower of Hollande, and it is arguable that Falorni got shabby treatment from his party when he was asked to step down in favor of the parachuted candidacy of Royal. But it appeared to

DOI: 10.1057/9781137356918.0008

be Trierweiler's jealousy of the president's former companion, Ségolène Royal, whom she had earlier pointedly excluded from some public functions, that was now on display for all to see. Was the new first lady taking her distance from the president in a show of independence? Was Hollande, on the other hand, au courant of (and thus complicit in) her intentions? Did her tweet deliver the "coup de grâce" to Royal's candidacy (polls showed Royal behind Forlani anyway, 58% to 42%)? However one answered these questions, and whether or not she took *Le Monde*'s advice to choose between her journalistic career and her functions as first lady and "forget Twitter," the "Affaire Trierweiler," "Premier Gaffe de France," or "Trierweilergate," or again, "Affaire Tweetweiler," did not seem likely to soon go away: the press, it was thought, would see to that. What remained to be seen was whether Hollande's "normal" presidency could resume. In fact Trierweiler made her apologies, and Hollande, in his news conference on July 14, declared that nothing like it would ever happen again. Trierweiler very quickly learned a lesson in discretion, and the "glass ceiling" so far as the French presidency is concerned remained in place.

The Socialist victory turned out to be historic in the sense that the Socialist Party's control over France was total, going beyond that achieved by François Mitterrand in 1981. The Socialists now had a majority not only in the National Assembly but in the Senate, too, which Mitterrand did not, and they controlled all but one of France's regions. They were in power in the vast majority of France's municipalities, including, of course, the city of Paris, which for years had been headed by the popular, gay mayor, Bernard Delanoë. It was, in fact, the total presidentialization of the regime, and Hollande seemed able to wield more power over his own country with less internal resistance than any other leader in Europe. It was not surprising that Prime Minister Ayrault, in his victory speech, emphasized strongly that France remained a parliamentary democracy, in which opposition parties retained full rights. Institutionally one might have wondered. Mitterrand himself once called the regime instituted by de Gaulle in 1958, "un coup d'État permanent." That might have been an exaggeration, but Hollande's overwhelming margin was the consequence of a political system that severely distorted the wishes of the electorate.[9] His own party, with 40% of the vote on the first ballot of the legislative elections, enjoyed a huge majority in the National Assembly. Bayrou and Le Pen between them had 27% of the vote on the first ballot of the presidential elections. Their parties ended up with two deputies each in the National Assembly, and neither was able to win a seat for himself or

DOI: 10.1057/9781137356918.0008

herself, nor for that matter could Mélenchon win a parliamentary seat. Hollande had pledged to modify the system, but that was one campaign promise he seemed unlikely to keep.

The primary reason for his probable reluctance remained the *Front national* of Marine Le Pen, which in this election managed a breakthrough by electing two or three deputies, depending on how one counts. In the Vaucluse, Marion Maréchal-Le Pen, the niece of Marine Le Pen, age 22, very young yet elegant and attractive, won in a "triangular" race, in which the Socialist candidate, who came in third, declined to stand down in favor of the better-placed UMP candidate in a "Republican Front" against the Right. Socialist policy was to desist on the second ballot where the FN was ahead and otherwise likely to win. The issue was further complicated in that the Socialist candidate who refused to stand down against Marion Le Pen was a Jewish woman, who maintained her candidacy despite the FN's known earlier anti-Semitism, arguing that even in defeat it was more important to show a left-wing presence in the department than to block Marion Le Pen. The other FN victories were those of an otherwise popular leader, Jacques Bompard, previously mayor of the town of Orange, in a rightist district of Marseille; and Gilbert Collard, a celebrity lawyer and writer, in the department of Gard. Bompard was not an FN member but was endorsed by the FN.

It also bears mentioning, that the imperfectly functioning "Republican Front" of the Socialists against the FN was not this time reciprocated by the UMP. Party leader François Copé, a ubiquitous presence on television's nightly news and later successor to Sarkozy as head of the UMP, rather trumpeted his party's "neither-nor" policy: the UMP would ally with neither the FN against the PS nor the PS against the FN, so long as the PS was willing to ally with the equally "extremist" Front de Gauche where the latter was best positioned for the second ballot against the UMP. The equation of the Front de Gauche by Copé with the FN rang hollow; the leftist group is neither a threat to the Republic, nor racist or anti-European.

The "neither-nor" policy of the UMP further masked a very troubling reality. Many members of the former governing party would have preferred a policy of cooperation with the National Front than to support the Socialists against them on the second ballot. In polls, more than a third of UMP voters said that they were more or less in agreement with the National Front and would prefer that their party cooperate with it.[10] At least one prominent UMP candidate made a point of appealing to their electorate by declaring that she shared their values. Sarkozy never dared to say as much (nor did Copé) but that was the former president's implicit message both during his campaign in 2007 and his desperate effort at reelection between rounds in 2012. But there are several obstacles to the FN cooperating with, infiltrating, or coming close to taking over the UMP, as the Tea Party appears on the verge of taking over the Republican Party in the United States. One obstacle is Europe, which the FN detests and to which the UMP must remain committed. The UMP represents France's major capitalist interests, and France is a globalized economy intimately bound up with the EU and its far-flung global role. The FN represents a frustrated petite bourgeoisie on the one hand (mostly in the South) and a displaced and formerly Communist working class on the other (mostly in the North).[11] It appears to have a shifting and unstable electorate. It also threatens to become the plaything of a politically ambitious but not overly intelligent family, with power being transmitted from Le Pen père to Le Pen fille, while Marine's niece, laughably at age 22 a deputy in the National Assembly, now its most prominent member of the younger generation.

Socialists in several parts of France do refuse to obey party dictates with impunity, the most prominent victim being in fact Ségolène Royal in her defeat by a dissenting Socialist in La Rochelle. The victorious Socialists could not control their own party in the end. But the irony of the victory stood out anyway in broad relief. It was the logical culmination of the house that de Gaulle built, his implicit goal of the monopolization of power by the Right, however, paradoxically now realized by the Left. The ultimate lesson of the election may be that the Fifth Republic, which has provided stable governments for France for more than 50 years since its creation in 1958, still remains fundamentally flawed and in need of revision. The party now in charge is the party that consistently criticized the system for its lack of democracy. To be sure, they did much to expand participation in the system through the institution of primaries and the promotion of women. But were they capable of reforming the system, or in winning back the lagging confidence of the voters in their leaders?

But the ultimate paradox of the election is that the all-powerful president Hollande is finding that his power is quite limited after all. It remains to be seen whether France is anything but another "no-choice" democracy, in other words a polity democratic in form and rights but bereft of political choices, the essential ones of which are made at the European Union level, or worse under pressure of the financial markets. To put it another way, there is a disconnect in Europe between policy

DOI: 10.1057/9781137356918.0008

and politics, legitimacy and responsibility. The states are still the locus of politics and legitimacy. But Europe is the maker of policy and the bearer of responsibility, under the watchful eye of the financial markets. The single most important economic statistic for any country in Europe today is neither its growth rate nor the number of its unemployed. It is rather the interest rate on its bonds.

Hollande's victory did at first appear to have shifted the locus of power in the EU. He seemed to have weakened the Franco-German tandem and empowered the Spanish and Italians as a consequence. The three Mediterranean countries acting together did pressure Mrs. Merkel into promising to accept a plan for mutual responsibility for Europe's banking system. In the Eurozone the banks are slated to come under a single jurisdiction and regulation system, with a Europe-wide or Euro-wide system of deposit insurance, akin to the FDIC in the United States, presumably in the offing. Hollande hoped to be a force within Europe. But what were his options in France? They appeared much more limited. France benefited at the moment from one of the lowest interest rates on its bonds in history, 2.5%. But this was not enough to allay fears about where it may go in the future. The total national debt was 90% of the yearly GNP, enough to frighten despite the low interest rate, and growth was stagnant or declining, enough to shake the "confidence" of the markets. Hollande was initially able to give the appearance of greater equity and justice in national politics. He diminished the salaries and perks of ministers and deputies and increased taxes on the rich, to a limit of 75% for the highest earners. However, a national consensus, to which Hollande also seemed committed, held that the debt needed to be reduced, which in turn meant that the annual budgetary deficit had to be eliminated. So rather than hiring new workers, the Socialist government committed itself to the continued firing of government officials, as Sarkozy had done. If the government added 60,000 education workers during the next five years, as promised, it would still have to fire as many in other departments. But this in turn would reverberate negatively on the unemployment situation, which remained at an alarmingly high level.

Hollande achieved three major goals in the Eurozone. He got his compact for growth and the appropriation of 130 billion euros from the European stabilization fund for investment in European infrastructure. He won consideration of a tax on financial transactions in the markets, which individual countries that use the Euro promised to implement immediately while all committed to do it eventually. And he got a commitment

DOI: 10.1057/9781137356918.0008

to an integrated European regulated banking system, although it was not yet clear how this was to be accomplished, and it faced much opposition. However, Hollande has had, in return, to accept the famous stabilization pact that forces all of Europe into the German straitjacket of balanced budgets in the future, with occasional deficits to be held at a maximum of 3% of GNP. Meanwhile, down the line there are fears for France's banks too. In the end, as Hollande proved incapable of separating the public and the private spheres in the case of the women in his life, he also appears unable to punch his way out of Sarkozy's and Merkel's shopping bag in terms of the economy. The "normal" presidency, despite appearances, may in time be able only to implement the same policies as its "abnormal" predecessor. The all-powerful president will need to show that he is not impotent before the power of the bankers and financiers.

Notes

1 Jerome Jaffré in Pascal Perrineau, *La Décision électorale en 2012* (Paris: Armand Colin, 2013), p. 209.

2 Laurent Binet, *Rien ne se passe comme prévu* (Paris: Grasset, 2012).

3 Jean-Luc Mano, *Les Phrases chocs de la campagne présidentielle* (Paris: Jean-Claude Gawsewitch, 2012), p. 12.

4 Nonna Mayer, personal interview.

5 Sineare and Cautrès, in Perrineau, *La Decision électorale*.

6 *Le Monde*, June 20, 2013.

7 *Le Monde*, June 21, 2012. See in particular the blog, "le 19 heures de François Fressoz: la fausse disparition de la gauche radicale."

8 "L'Affaire Trierweiler," *Le Nouvel Observateur*, June 14, 2012.

9 Historian Eric Roussel, in contrast to political scientists like Perrineau and Badie, who emphasize issues in France's political crisis, points to the nature of the institutions of the Fifth Republic established by de Gaulle in 1958, and still in effect. Personal interview, June 19, 2011.

10 Pascal Perrineau, *Le Choix de Marianne : Pourquoi et pour qui votons nous?* (Paris: Fayard, 2012).

11 Mayer and Perrineau both make this point. See Pascal Perrineau, *Le Symptôme Le Pen: Radiographie des électeurs du Front national* (Paris: Fayard, 1997).

DOI: 10.1057/9781137356918.0008

Conclusion

Abstract: *The presidency of François Hollande got off to an inauspicious start. Despite an initial spurt of reforms, including gay marriage, Hollande's popularity plummeted, faster and to levels lower than any other president in French history. The economy worsened, and the government failed to reverse the downward spiral of employment. Hollande failed to renegotiate the stability pact of the Eurozone, forcing his majority instead to ratify it despite opposition. The growth fund was too little and had no discernible effect. Hollande imposed even greater austerity than his predecessor in an attempt to balance the budget, or bring the deficit down to the Eurozone required level of 3% of GDP. The political crisis worsened, the National Front surged in support, and the government was badly defeated in municipal elections, a UMP sweep in which the National Front candidates became mayors of ten important cities. France appeared to be a no-choice if not endangered democracy.*

Wall, Irwin. *France Votes: The Election of François Hollande.* New York: Palgrave Macmillan, 2014. DOI: 10.1057/9781137356918.0009.

DOI: 10.1057/9781137356918.0009

A year and a half into his presidency, by the beginning of 2014, François Hollande could congratulate himself on the successful implementation of many or most of his campaign promises. Among them, gay marriage stood out by its surprise provocation of vocal opposition among devout Catholics, who had previously been unheard from in political demonstrations since Mitterrand had threatened the system of aid to Catholic schools in 1983. Gay couples, according to the law on the family, also received the right to adopt children. The retirement system was reformed, along with the system of teacher training. While the reformed pension system in the end hardly elicited great excitement among the public, the rights of special categories of workers to retire at age 60 was upheld. Universities received promised greater autonomy. Hollande turned over the right of appointments of the heads of public television and radio to the councils of those agencies, whereas Sarkozy had arrogated these appointments to himself. This was a blow for greater freedom of public information. And after a year and a half of struggle, the National Assembly finally abolished the practice of parliamentary representatives and senators to accumulate offices on the local level. It was estimated that up to 80% of French parliamentarians simultaneously served as mayors, departmental and municipal councilors, or held other local offices in their districts. This was one of the political practices, long enshrined in French politics since the 19th century, that was thought to contribute to the sense of political crisis in France; its end was almost unanimously applauded as a victory for democratic practice.

Other measures were at least partially implemented or on the way toward adoption: the 75% tax on incomes over one million euros was initially rejected by the constitutional court and then reduced to 66.7% taking into account other taxes already in place, but it was sufficient to cause Gerard Depardieu to seek citizenship first in Belgium, and then finally in Russia, where President Putin, once a Communist, promised the French actor the maximum protections of his accumulated fortune from threat of government confiscation. French soccer teams loudly protested that the 75% income tax rate meant they would be unable to hire competitive players, and other entertainers protested as well, but the government held firm. The National Assembly adopted harsher punishments for fiscal fraud.

The government made a show of attacking the problem of unemployment: it created "emplois d'avenir," government subsidized jobs for disadvantaged youth for up to three years in what might be regarded

DOI: 10.1057/9781137356918.0009

as internships, the holders of which presumably acquired skills leading to jobs in the future. By October 2013 it appeared that the government would achieve its goal of creating 100,000 such jobs by the end of the year. And it further subsidized *"contrats de génération,"* generational labor contracts that enabled workers approaching retirement age to employ alongside them younger workers to learn from them on the job and assure the transmission of skills. However, this reform got off to a slower start; only 11,000 such jobs were created in the first 8 months after the law was passed. In all a breakdown of all the promises held and broken published by *Le Monde* showed that about half of Hollande's 60 campaign promises had been implemented. Considering that the government still enjoyed years in power ahead of it, it was possible to take satisfaction in what had been accomplished. Moreover the reforms were popular.

But however well-intentioned the government seemed, it was powerless to turn around the economy. The most important of Hollande's promises was to reverse the upward trend of unemployment by jump starting the economy. But quarter after quarter the figures were deceiving, and in his New Year's address of 2014 Hollande had formally to admit that he had as yet been unable to fulfill that most important of promises. The economy had continued to stagnate or contract since his election, unemployment reached 11.1%, and another 177,000 jobs had been lost. More than three million workers were without jobs, youth unemployment was at 25%, and rates of 50% were common in suburbs largely inhabited by minorities and the poor. With the economy in virtual depression Hollande continued to inhabit the lowest depths in presidential polls in French history, with 24% of the French approving his performance as president and 76% disapproving.[1] His prime minister, Ayrault, languished equally at a dismal 25% favorable rating. Most alarmingly, 51% of Socialist voters fell into the negative camp on Hollande. Nor would the numbers bottom out. By the time of the municipal elections in March 2014 Hollande's favorability rating had fallen to 17%.[2]

Hollande's fall from grace had been the most rapid and steep in French history; by December 2012, in little more than six months, he fell from a momentary high of 61% favorability rating to 40%, with 59% of the French pronouncing themselves dissatisfied with their president's performance thus far. French pessimism continued unabated: the single event that most overjoyed the nation during 2012 was not their own election result but rather the election of Barack Obama.[3] Hollande's free fall continued into 2013, falling to 25% favorability rating in April and 20%

DOI: 10.1057/9781137356918.0009

in October.[4] No president had ever fallen below 30% in French opinion polls since the establishment of the Fifth Republic. Sarkozy reached 30%, a historic low to that point, in April 2011, but he recovered to 40% by the time of the elections.[5] In contrast, since hitting his low of 20%, Hollande has remained near that level into 2014.

Pascal Perrineau offered three basic explanations for the unprecedented rapidity and steepness of Hollande's fall from grace. The first was a tax increase that despite denials by the government fell largely on the middle class. To be sure, the rhetoric behind the increase was that it focused on those most able to pay. On the one hand there was the famous 75% on incomes above one million euros per year; on the other hand there was also the creation of new category and tax rate involving an increase for those with incomes over 150,000 euros per year. These changes allegedly left 90% of the French with their circumstances unchanged. But this argument was a bit disingenuous; the Sarkozy government had frozen the indexation of taxes according to inflation.[6] Previously the tax scale was adjusted for inflation so that those receiving more cash income were shielded from falling into higher brackets by taxing only their increases in real income, purchasing power, as opposed to nominally higher cash income. Hollande had pledged to abolish the freeze but instead, under pressure to bring the budget closer into balance, he continued it. Thus all taxpayers felt an increased bite out of their incomes, while at the same time an increase in the TVA, the "value added tax" that functions like a sales tax, further depressed rather than increased purchasing power.

Second, as the months wore on the unemployment rate increased and the depression deepened. Hollande pled for patience; he had only promised to turn the falling rate of employment around during 2013, by which time his policies would have a chance to work. But meanwhile it became clear to voters that the new president could not or would not implement those policies. During the campaign Hollande had emphasized a new politics of growth taken to the Eurozone level. He pledged to renegotiate the stability pact to include a clause related to growth in step with ending the politics of austerity. However, the Germans would not renegotiate the pact; they would agree only to a letter accompanying its signing to stipulate that a growth fund of 130 billion euros would be established. As a stimulus measure to be parceled out over the economies of 17 countries this was sadly insufficient to achieve the desired result. The American stimulus of 2009, for example, was over 800 billion dollars in an economy of equivalent size, and it was rapidly judged insufficient by economists like Krugman and Stieglitz. Having achieved his growth package, itself ephemeral (according to some analysts 55 billion consisted of existing projects, the funds for which were simply redirected to the growth package), Hollande agreed to French ratification of the stability pact. On the Left it appeared that austerity had again very quickly raised its ugly head. Mélenchon quickly denounced the treaty and declared he would vote against it. The Greens also objected, and there were protests on the left of the PS, with open anger being expressed against Merkel and the Germans. Meanwhile Daniel Cohn-Bendit, putative leader of Europe's Green Party, observed that having been elected with France's environmentalist voters solidly in his camp, Hollande proceeded to ignore them.[7]

To complicate things further, the government shrank from its initial promise to prevent the partial closure of the steelworks at Florange, where Hollande had publicly campaigned in February 2012. Budgetary problems and EU regulations stood in the way of nationalization; instead the government agreed to closure of the blast furnaces in exchange for the continuation of the plant operations on finished steel. Some jobs were saved. But a similarly ineffective effort to rescue a Goodyear tire plant threatened with closure and accompanying loss of jobs revealed Hollande's campaign promises to have been empty of content. Peugeot, the French auto company, closed its plant outside Paris at Aulnay. On October 1, 2012, there was a demonstration in Paris against the stability pact, labeled the "Traité Merkozy" by demonstrators. Hollande found himself, according to *Le Monde*, "outflanked, overwhelmed, by his left" (*débordé par la gauche*).[8] Hollande was trapped by circumstances into deceiving his followers. The French, in electing him, voted against austerity and Hollande campaigned against austerity while promising to balance the budget too. But 64% of the French favored the stability treaty, and 72% believed at the same time in the necessity of a balanced budget enshrined in law, the so-called *règle d'or budgétaire* or budgetary golden rule.

Perrineau also thought Hollande would have done better to postpone the question of gay marriage. The sequence of demonstrations and protests it evoked, however, were unforeseen, and it enjoys a majority in French opinion and represented fulfillment of a campaign promise. Proponents campaigned for it with the clever slogan "*Mariage pour tous*," marriage for everyone, leading to the formation of an opposition group, "*La manif pour tous*," protests for everyone, in November 2012

DOI: 10.1057/9781137356918.0009

in opposition to the introduction of the legislation in the National Assembly. *La manif pour tous,* led by a humorist who for the occasion called herself "Frigide Barjot," successfully organized some very large demonstrations in November 2012 and January 2013 involving hundreds of thousands of people. They revealed a core of militant Catholic opinion otherwise unexpressed in contemporary French politics; notably the National Front declined to participate, remaining neutral on the subject, in deference perhaps to the fact that 65% of the French favor gay marriage according to the polls. The disturbances wrought by the legislation may well have contributed to Hollande's flagging popularity, but the bill enjoyed broad support. The UMP protested and brought it before the constitutional council, but that body proclaimed it constitutional and Hollande promulgated it as law in April 2013.

It is likely that Hollande himself is in large part the cause of his own lack of popularity. He is uninspiring as a leader and projects hesitancy and uncertainty in his approach to issues. On television, during the campaign, he projected a surprising personal strength and shone in his debate with Sarkozy. But in post-election press conferences, of which there have been few, he appeared timid, almost shy. The slogan of the "normal" president likely did not help. There has been a certain desacralization of the French presidency that began with Sarkozy, and Hollande seems determined to continue the process. French presidents until Sarkozy, De Gaulle, Pompidou, Giscard d'Estaing, Mitterrand, and Chirac, all seemed to manage a kind of regal bearing in imitation of de Gaulle who was very much a "republican monarch." In projecting normalcy in opposition to Sarkozy's frenetic style Hollande may have meant that he would restore the office's dignity, but his personal bearing failed to do so. The French appear to have viewed the president as rather like themselves, and perhaps a new generation prefers that in a president. But in a crowd in Dijon in March 2013 Hollande was peppered with questions and accusations about his politics of the Right, blamed for having done nothing in nine months, asked "where are your campaign promises," and bluntly told to get rid of Valérie, as "we don't like her."[9] (This last was a rather bizarre request which to everyone's surprise Hollande was to carry out at year's end.)

Hollande did show a surprising boldness in foreign policy that was unexpected and which received American plaudits. "Françafrique" is a loaded term that once designated more or less French colonial sub-Saharan or black Africa in which the French retained post-colonial influence, whether economic or cultural, and protected their interests by maintaining a military force there to keep in power a corrupt network of dictators tied to France. The once-labeled "ministry of cooperation" that no longer exists was in fact a ministry for Africa. Hollande pledged to put an end to Françafrique in the traditional sense; the French presence would remain but in the interest of democracy and development, not the preservation of corrupt colonial interests. If France intervened, it would be in cooperation and alongside other African states and with the authorization of the United Nations.

Mali came under threat from Al Qaeda in North Africa as a kind of spillover of the events in Libya. The overthrow of Gadaffi enabled radical Islamists to get a foothold in the region, where discontent reigned among Tuareg peoples who sought autonomy or independence from blacks in the south, in alliance with who the Jihadists threatened the Malian regime to the south. Timbuktu fell; lives were lost and cultural treasures there were pillaged while sharia was enforced. The French intervention was decided in a matter of days, and it quickly turned the tide against the rebels. Hollande showed uncharacteristic boldness in foreign policy, scoring a quick success in public opinion. He received the logistical support of the United States, but France at the outset was going it alone, and like most interventions, once in Mali the French could not easily see how they would get out. But Hollande was undeterred. In Syria he demanded that Assad leave power; during his campaign he threatened swift retribution if the Syrian dictator resorted to chemical weapons. Once elected, Hollande went to Moscow in an effort to convince the Russians to cease their support for the Syrian regime, coming home empty-handed, however.

These efforts came to naught, but Hollande also showed a certain independence from Washington as well, supporting Palestine in its bid for United Nations membership. On the other hand the Americans took no umbrage at this; some speculated that they were secretly glad to see the Europeans vote in the UN as they would have wished to do themselves. Hollande visited Israel to show support for the country but firmly demanded Palestinian independence and a two-state solution while he was there. In relations with the United States Hollande continued the policies begun by Sarkozy, who had ended the estrangement between the two countries over the Iraq Wars and brought the French back into NATO after a 50-year hiatus, during which France had remained in the alliance but shunned participation in the NATO integrated command.

DOI: 10.1057/9781137356918.0009

Sarkozy was thought to be very pro-American, but sources in the Quai say that his enthusiasm for Franco-American cooperation waned somewhat toward the end of his administration, when participation in NATO's integrated command did not yield a stronger role for and consultation of France in the alliance. This did not prevent the American embassy from insisting, after Hollande's election, that French-American relations were the best they had ever been since the Second World War.[10] If there is not genuine friendship between Obama and Hollande, Obama appreciates Hollande as being much more serious and reliable than was Sarkozy, while Kerry who speaks French perfectly gets along extremely well with Laurent Fabius.[11] There is full cooperation between the two countries in dealing with the terrorist threat. They see eye to eye on Syria as well, although France recognizes the Syrian opposition as a provisional government while Washington does not. Having promised to deal firmly with the threat of chemical weapons in Syria, Hollande offered immediate and full support when Obama threatened to bombard the country after receiving confirmed reports that the weapons had been used. After Obama backed down, however, Hollande suffered something of a setback.

Although a permanent member of the United Nations Security Council, France counts for little in world affairs, and Europe is the focus of most of its action and intention. Europe, more specifically Germany and Angela Merkel, held the key to the implementation of Hollande's policies. Hollande was frustrated in his desire for Eurobonds, in which many observers see the means of saving the euro. He wanted a politics of growth to balance the politics of austerity in the EU, while he attempted to combine budget balancing with stimulus for growth at home. He got none of these things. And with his competitiveness pact, in which he sought to alleviate the heavy social charges on French businesses, he seemed to have repudiated his earlier views in any case, announcing that he was a devotee of "supply-side economics" (*une politique d'offre*). For *Le Monde* this was not simply an example of a slide toward neo-liberalism but a real break with the Socialist economics of the past.[12]

Hollande promised not only a more normal presidency but moral governance. However, only a few months into his presidency, his finance minister, a former cosmetic-surgeon-turned-financier, Jérôme Cahuzac, brazenly denied ever having had a Swiss bank account and then was forced to admit his lie when Mediapart, the web-based

DOI: 10.1057/9781137356918.0009

newspaper in France, offered proof. Suspicion pointed at Hollande; if he knew, he had hidden it. If he did not know, he was incompetent. Hollande evinced his own corporate ties: his chief of staff (*Directrice du cabinet*) Sylvie Hubac is a fellow graduate of the ENA, married to Philippe Crouzet, CEO of the industrial giant Vallourec and one of the richest men in France. But worse, critics wondered whether Cahuzac did not represent the tip of the iceberg, the bulk of government venality and corruption remaining hidden as always. Hollande had promised reform to make government transparent and worthy of the trust of its citizens. Instead, one year into his presidency, the resignation of his budget minister left the nation's political crisis, the disaffection between its political class and its citizens, deeper than ever.[13] In desperation, Hollande forced his ministers to disclose all their holdings and the banks their foreign deposits.

But the final indignity struck in the arena in which Hollande had made so much capital at Sarkozy's expense. If the French could not forgive Sarkozy's mixing of the personal and the political they were even less tolerant of Hollande's version of *Le roi s'amuse*. Like the French kings before him Hollande had his mistress; or was it two mistresses, since the female inhabitant of the Elysée was not his wife to begin with? And if it amused the president-king to ride clandestinely on his motorcycle around Paris, helmeted as much for privacy as for safety, on visits to his newest lady-love (the film actress, Julie Gayet), it did not add to his luster. The Elysée briefly became the scene of a soap opera when the "first lady" collapsed in distress and had to be hospitalized. Nor was the manner of her undoing amusing: Hollande, after defending his right to privacy at a news conference, was asked whether Valérie Trierweiler was still the first lady. His answer was that he would issue a clarification soon. And indeed, he did: she was no longer first lady. The office was vacant if it ever existed.

Hollande's fall in popular opinion was evident in the municipal elections that took place on May 23, 2014. The PS suffered a severe defeat. The Socialists got 43% of the total vote, the UMP 48%. The National Front received 5% but fielded candidates in only 600 of the nation's 36,000 municipalities. On the local level this meant serious breakthroughs for the party which showed that it had become a national force. Indeed, it went on to get 25% in European elections in May, allowing it to claim that it was now the leading party in France. In Hénin-Beaumont, once a communist bastion, now a stronghold of

DOI: 10.1057/9781137356918.0009

the FN, Marine Le Pen lost her race for a National Assembly seat by 1% in 2012, but two years later the party won the mayoralty with a majority on the first ballot. The FN remained well positioned on the second ballot in several of the larger cities of France. Meanwhile the abstention rate in these elections hit an all-time high for municipal elections in France, 38%.[14]

The second ballot of the municipal elections saw the UMP take back from the PS a majority of the cities and towns of France with populations over 10,000. The PS was able to hold on to Paris, where a woman, Anne Hidalgo, the first female mayor of Paris, won election, and in Lyon, where the popular Gérard Colomb, in office since 2001, won yet another term. Strasbourg was another PS bright spot. But the PS was defeated in Toulouse, and in other relatively important cities like Quimper, Reims, and Amiens. More significant perhaps than the overwhelming UMP victory was the fact that in the 244 communes where it ran, the Front National showed deep implantation, its voters remaining loyal to it between rounds. Indeed the party got a higher percentage on the second ballot, 18.6% of the vote, as opposed to 17.3% on the first ballot. And if the total percentage of the FN vote was similar to the totals it received in the presidential elections two years before, the FN was nevertheless able to win the mayoralties of ten cities of over 10,000 inhabitants, including Hénin-Baumont, Fréjus, and Béziers, while its candidates racked up totals of 48% in Saint Gilles and 45% in Perpignan, and over 30% in 32 of the other 244 cities it contested in. More ominously, in towns where its candidates seemed better placed to win on the second ballot, the FN for the first time in its history was able to increase its totals between rounds, from 34.5% to 40.9% of the vote, attracting UMP voters who preferred it to the Socialists, while FN voters similarly voted for UMP voters better placed against the PS on the second round. What this showed was that if the UMP and FN continued to despise one another their voters did not; and Marine Le Pen's campaign of "de-diabolization" was apparently having an effect. The FN is likely to remain a major force in French politics on the local, national, and European levels for the foreseeable future.[15]

Thus we have a stinging defeat for Hollande and the PS which has lost most of France's major cities to the Right. A serious menacing breakthrough on the local level as the FN becomes for the first time, in the words of Marine Le Pen, a government party. And the FN has become the largest French party on the level of the European Union, which it despises. All this adds up to new evidence of the growing disaffection of the electorate from all the choices offered them by democratic politics in France today.

The "normal" president was not so normal after all. Yet in the end neither corruption nor dalliance with women is likely to determine the outcome of his presidency. France remains mired in a neo-liberal morass. Purchasing power continues to decline while unemployment continues to rise. A system of excessive public debt financed by banks appears to require a kind of institutionalized system of austerity as a remedy.[16] But no matter how much the government cuts its public services it cannot keep up with the declining rate of its receipts. Inequality continues to grow, with increasing profits yet stagnant or declining wages. The European Union is a system of untrammeled competition, not mutual cooperation. It offers its ailing members exhortations about competiveness in place of support, and requires further austerity in exchange for its bail-outs. Hollande seems caught in a vicious circle identical to the one that consigned his predecessor to failure. Whether he can find his way out during his presidency seems in question. Meanwhile the politics of populism, neo-nationalism, and extremism flourish. France's political crisis remains far from resolution.

Notes

1   *Le Parisien,* January 13, 2014.
2   *Le Point,* March 6, 2014.
3   Denis Merzet, *La France des illusions perdues* (Paris: Editions de l'Aube, 2013), pp. 50–62. The title of this collection of essays itself speaks volumes about the atmosphere in the country following the election.
4   *Le Monde,* October 9, 2013.
5   «Impopularité de Nicolas Sarkozy : retour sur un quinquennat,» *Le nouvel Observateur,* April 13, 2012.
6   *Le Figaro,* September 11, 2012.
7   Daniel Cohn-Bendit, in Merzet, *La France des illusions perdues,* pp. 62–77.
8   *Le Monde,* October 1, 2012.
9   "La familiarité, prix de la normalité," *Le Monde,* March 23, 2013.
10 Personal interview, Alexander Schrank, American Embassy, Paris, June 6, 2013.
11 Personal interview, Quai d'Orsay, June 17, 2013.

DOI: 10.1057/9781137356918.0009

12 Camille Jouve, *Un an après l'élection de François Hollande : tableau d'un glissement néolibéral* (Paris: Editons Syllepse, 2013). *Le Monde*, November 15, 2012.

13 Cynthie Fleury, in Merzet, *La France des illusions perdues.*

14 *Le Monde*, May 24, 2014.

15 Institut Français d'Opinion Publique (IFOP), Focus. «Premières analyses du FN au 2nd tour des municipales.»

16 Jouve, *Un an après l'élection de François Hollande*, passim, pp. 40–42, 56–58, 111–113.

DOI: 10.1057/9781137356918.0009

Appendix

French election, 2012

Candidate	Party	Popular Vote	Percentage
First ballot, April 22, 2012			
François Hollande	PS (Socialist)	10,272,705	28.63
Nicolas Sarkozy	UMP (Union for a Popular Movement Conservative)	9,753,629	27.18
Marine Le Pen	National Front (Far Right)	6,421,426	17.90
Jean-Luc Mélenchon			
	Front de Gauche (Far Left)	3,984,822	11.1
François Bayrou	Democratic Movement (Center)	3,275,122	9.13
Eva Joly	Europe, Ecology, Greens	828,345	2.31
Nicolas Dupont-Aignan	Conservative (Anti- Europe)	643,907	1.79
Philippe Poutou	Extreme Left	411,160	1.15
Nathalie Arthaud	Trotskyist	202,548	0.44
Jacques Cheminade	Libertarian	89,545	0.19
Second ballot, May 6, 2012			
François Hollande		18,000,668	51.64
Nicolas Sarkozy		16,860,685	48.64

TABLE II *French elections: legislative, first ballot, June 10, 2012*

Party	Seats Won	Vote Total	Percentage
PS (Socialist)	22	7,618,326	29.35
UMP (Conservative)	9	7,037,268	27.12
National Front		3,528,663	13.60
Front de Gauche		1,793,192	6.91
Europe, Ecology, Green	1	1,418,264	5.46
Misc. Right	1	910,034	3.51
Misc. Left	1	881,555	3.40
New Center	1	569,897	2.20
MoDem (Center)		458,098	1.77
Left Radicals	1	428,898	1.65

DOI: 10.1057/9781137356918.0010

TABLE III   *French legislative elections, second ballot, June 17, 2012 (541 of 577 districts voting)*

Party	Seats Won	Popular Vote*	Percentage of Vote*
PS (Socialists)	258	9,420,889	40.91
UMP (Conservative)	185	8,740,628	37.95
Front National	3		
Front de Gauche	10		
Radicals	6		
Europe, Ecology, Green	16		
Left Radicals	11		
Misc. Left	21		
MoDem	2		
Misc. Right	14		
New Center	11		
Regionalists	2		
Center Alliance	2		

* Only the vote totals of the major parties are presented here. Second ballot results in each district are heavily dependent on first ballot results and alliances concluded between the ballots. The numbers and percentages of the vote received by the minor parties represent only those districts in which they were able to present second-ballot candidates and are therefore of limited importance and are not presented here.

DOI: 10.1057/9781137356918.0010

Bibliography

Aghion, Philippe. « Comment redresser l'économie française, » *La Revue Socialiste* (45–46, 2011).

Aghion, Philippe and Roulet, Alexandre. *Repenser l'Etat : Pour une socialedémocratie de l'innovation*. Paris: Seuil, 2011.

Anderson, Perry. *The New Old World*. London: Verso Books, 2011.

Arestis, Phillip and Sawyer, Malcolm, eds. *The Euro Crisis*. New York: Palgrave Macmillan, 2012.

Askenazy, Philippe and Cohen, Daniel, eds. *16 Nouvelles questions d'économie contemporaine*. Paris: Albin Michel, 2010.

Bacqué, Raphaëlle and Chemin, Ariane. *Les Strauss-Kahn*. Paris: Albin Michel, 2012.

Badie, Bertrand. *Un monde sans souveraineté : les Etats entre ruse et responsabilité*. Paris: Fayard, 1999.

Bavarez, Nicolas. *La France qui tombe : Un constat clinique du déclin français*. Paris: Perrin, 2003.

Bercoff, André. *Moi, Président...* Paris: Editions First-Gründ, 2013.

Binet, Laurent. *Rien ne se passe comme prévu*. Paris: Grasset, 2012.

Blythe, Marc. *Austerity: The History of a Dangerous Idea*. Oxford: Oxford University Press, 2013.

Bouilhaguet, Alix and Jakubyszyn, Aristophe. *La Frondeuse*. Paris: Editions du Moment, 2012.

Cotta, Michel. *Le rose et le gris*. Paris: Fayard, 2012.

Davies, Peter. *The National Front in France: Ideology, Discourse and Power*. London: Routledge, 1999.

DOI: 10.1057/9781137356918.0011

Dézé, Alexandre. *Le Front National : à la conquête du pouvoir?* Paris: Armand Colin, 2012.

Dockès, Pierre and Lorenzi, Jean-Hervé. *Fin de Monde ou sortie de crise.* Paris: Perrin, 2009.

Duhamel, Olivier and Lacerf, Edouard, eds. *L'Etat d'opinion, 2013.* Paris: Seuil, 2013.

Dupin, Éric. *La victoire empoisonnée : et maintenant?* Paris: Seuil, 2012.

Epstein, Beth. *Collective Terms: Race, Culture & Community in a State-Planned City in France.* London and New York: Berghahn Books, 2011.

Epstein, Edward Jay. What Really Happened to Strauss-Kahn. *The New York Review of Books,* December 22, 2011.

Estier, Claude. *Journal d'une victoire.* Paris: Cherche-Midi, 2012.

Federbusch, Serge. *l'enfumeur.* Paris: Editions Ixelles, 2013.

Gillingham, John. *European Integration, 1950–2003: Superstate or New Market Economy?* Cambridge: Cambridge University Press, 2003.

Gourevitch, Philip. Can Nicolas Sarkozy—and France—Survive the European Crisis? *The New Yorker,* September 12, 2011.

Haegel, Florence. *Les Droites en fusion ; Transformations de l'UMP.* Paris: Presses de la Fondation Nationale des Sciences Politiques, 2012.

Jankowski, Paul. *Shades of Indignation: Political Scandals in France Past and Present.* New York: Berghahn Books, 2008.

Jouve, Camille. *Un an après l'élection de François Hollande : tableau d'un glissement néolibéral.* Paris: Editons Syllepse, 2013.

Kahn, Jean-François. *Comment s'en sortir.* Paris: Plon, 2013.

—. *La Catastrophe du 6 Mai 2012.* Paris: Plon, 2012.

Lorenzi, Jean-Hervé. *La Fabuleuse destin d'une puissance intermédiaire.* Paris: Grasset, 2011.

Maclean, Meiri and Szarka, Joseph, eds. *France on the World Stage.* New York: Palgrave Macmillan, 2008.

Malouines, Marie-Eve. *La force du gentil.* Paris: JC Lattès, 2012.

Mano, Jean-Luc. *Les Phrases chocs de la campagne présidentielle.* Paris: Jean-Claude Gawsewitch, 2012.

Mansouret, Anne. *Chronique d'une victoire avortée.* Paris: Jean-Claude Gawsewitch, 2011.

Mayer, Nonna. *Ces Français qui votent Le Pen.* Paris: Flammarion, 2002.

Mayer, Nonna and Pascal Perrineau, eds. *Le Front National à Découvert.* Paris: Presses de la Fondation Nationale des Sciences Politiques, 1989.

Merzet, Denis, ed. *La France des illusions perdues.* Paris: Editions de l'Aube, 2013.

DOI: 10.1057/9781137356918.0011

Mexandeau, Louis. *Histoire du P.S. (1905–2005)*. Paris: Tallendier, 2005.

Michel, Richard. *François Hollande, l'inattendu*. Paris: L'Archipel, 2011.

Monnot, Caroline and Mestre, Abel. *La système Le Pen : Enquête sur les reseaux du FN*. Paris: Denoël, 2011.

Morrison, Donald and Compagnon, Antoine. *The Death of French Culture*. New York: Polity Press, 2010.

Moss, Bernard. *Monetary Union in Crisis: The European Union as a Neo-Liberal Construction*. New York: Palgrave Macmillan, 2005.

Murray, Rainbow. *Parties, Gender Quotas, and Candidate Selection in France*. Paris: Palgrave Macmillan, 2010.

Opollo, Katherine. *Gender Quotas, Parity Reform, and Political Parties in France*. Lanham, MD: Lexington Books, 2006.

Perrineau, Pascal. *Le Choix de Marianne : Pourquoi et pour qui votons nous?* Paris: Fayard, 2012.

———, ed. *La Décision électorale en 2012*. Paris: Armand Colin, 2013.

Perrineau, Pascal and Rouban, Luc, eds. *La Solitude de l'isoloir: Les vrais enjeux de 2012*. Paris: Presses de la Fondation Nationale des Sciences Politiques, 2012.

———. *Le Symptôme Le Pen : Radiographie des électeurs du Front national*. Paris: Fayard, 1997.

———. *Le vote de rupture : les elections presidentielles et legislatives d'avril-juin, 2008*. Paris: Presses de la Fondation Nationale des Sciences Politiques, 2008.

———. *Politics in France and Europe*. New York: Palgrave Macmillan, 2009.

Piketty, Thomas. *Capital in the 21st Century*. Cambridge: Harvard University Press, 2014.

Reymond, Gino, ed. *The Sarkozy Presidency: Breaking the Mold*. New York: Palgrave Macmillan, 2013.

Schain, Martin. *The Politics of Immigration in France, Britain, and the United States*. New York: Palgrave Macmillan, 2008; second edition, 2012.

Scott, Joan. *Parité*. Chicago: University of Chicago Press, 2005.

Sutton, Michael. *France and the Construction of Europe, 1944–2007*. New York: Berghahn Books, 2007.

Sylvestre, Jean-Marc. *On nous ment : Verités et légendes sur la crise*. Paris: Fayard, 2011.

Wall, Irwin. France Votes. *French Politics, Culture and Society*, Vol. 30, No. 3 (Fall 2012), 1–20.

DOI: 10.1057/9781137356918.0011

Index

DOI: 10.1057/9781137356918.0012

DOI: 10.1057/9781137356918.0012

DOI: 10.1057/9781137356918.0012

DOI: 10.1057/9781137356918.0012

CPSIA information can be obtained at www.ICGtesting.com
Printed in the USA
LVOW10*1535120914

403819LV00001B/2/P